A Vision from the South

Mercio Gomes,
Chandra Kirana,
Sami Songanbele & Rajiv Vora

A Vision from the South

How wealth degrades the environment:
sustainability in the Netherlands

This book is a project of ANPED,
Alliance of Northern Peoples for Environment and Development
& the Dutch Alliance for Sustainable Development

International Books, Uitgeverij Jan van Arkel, 1992
World Information Service on Environment and Development
(WISE)

The publication of this book was made possible by a grant from the Ministry of Housing, Physical Planning and Environmental Management (VROM)

The "Vision" Project has been funded by
Nationale Postcode Loterij (NPL)
Directoraat Generaal Internationale Samenwerking (DGIS)
Nationale Commissie Voorlichting en Bewustwording
–Ontwikkelingssamenwerking (NCO)
Wereld Natuur Fonds (WNF)
Humanistisch Instituut voor Ontwikkelingssamenwerking (HIVOS)

First published in 1992 by International Books, an imprint of Uitgeverij Jan van Arkel, A. Numankade 17, 3572 KP Utrecht, the Netherlands.

Mercio Gomes et. al.
A Vision from the South
How wealth degrades environment: sustainability in the Netherlands / by Mercio Gomes, Chandra Kirana, Sami Songanbele, Rajiv Vora: [photos.: diverse sources] - Utrecht: Jan van Arkel
ISBN: 90 6224 994 9

Cover photos: Ruud Gort, Amsterdam
Cover design: Optima Forma, Nijmegen
Inside printwork: Bariet, Ruinen
Cover printing: Thieme, Nijmegen
Photographs: Ruud Gort, Evert Boeve, Hollandse Hoogte (HH)

Contents

Forewords & Acknowledgements   7

Introduction
Mercio Gomes   17

Chapter 1
In search of sustainability
Rajiv Vora   25

Chapter 2
Dutch environment as they see it
Mercio Gomes   47

Chapter 3
Agriculture, transport, and industry
Sami Songambele   69

Chapter 4
Hard problems, soft solutions
Chandra Kirana   93

Chapter 5
Can Dutch society put limits on itself?
Rajiv Vora   109

Epilogue
Mercio Gomes, Chandra Kirana, Sami Songambele, Rajiv Vora   121

Bibliography   127

Foreword from the Alliance of Northern Peoples for Environment and Development

The Alliance appreciates the initiative taken by WISE and the four Southern consultants. We realize that it is important to reverse the usual development analysis of the South by the North, and we welcome this fresh look at our societies. We accept the challenge of the central conclusion in this book, that the North "will have to cut down on its life style of over-production and over-consumption". The Alliance will promote this analysis in other Northern countries, and we undertake to bring A Vision from the South to the attention of our member organizations, other interested bodies and the general public.

Clare Flenley
Alliance of Northern Peoples for Environment and Development (ANPED)

Foreword from The Alliance for Sustainable Development

When WISE approached the Alliance for Sustainable Development with the idea of inviting people from the South to write a critical report on the sustainability of Dutch society, we were immediately enthusiastic. Sustainable development, an integrated vision on environment, development, peace and security, is a central element within the work of the Alliance. And within the Alliance it is strongly felt that the voice from the South is very important in the discussion on sustainable development. This project offers us a unique possibility, because now it is people from the South who criticize our society from their perspective. A change of direction within the usual reality in which the North lets its critical light shine on the "development" of the South.

The Alliance is, as coordinator of the inputs of the non-governmental organizations (NGOs) of the Netherlands, involved with the preparation of UNCED. A central activity in this coordination is the writing of a national NGO report. In that report, the Dutch NGOs working on environment, development, peace and security, describe their vision and perspective on a sustainable Netherlands. The discussion on this report is now in progress. *A Vision from the South* is well timed. It will enrich the discussion on our own national report and strengthen our thinking on sustainable development.

In a discussion with members of the Alliance, one of the four guests from the South indicated appreciation of the value we place in the vision from the South.

"It is," she said, "An important step in the right direction."

"But," she added, "we will only be equal if we will be able to give our opinion of you without being asked."

The Alliance for Sustainable Development thanks the guests from the South for giving us their opinion on the sustainable Netherlands. We also thank the people who supported and guided the project. The Alliance recognizes the challenge of this report in the discussion on sustainable development and will do its utmost to give it the fullest attention in the preparations of the UNCED.

Frans Bauke van der Meer
Chairperson of the Alliance for Sustainable Development

Foreword from WISE

The aim of WISE is to link organizations and individuals who are active on issues relating to environment and development. WISE staff collect information, organize conferences and seminars and write reports on themes such as forestry, agriculture, climate, the debt crisis and resource conflicts. WISE also publishes a bi-weekly news communique which links activists around the world campaigning against nuclear energy and for safe alternatives.

WISE projects cross not only geographical borders, but also cultural and ideological borders. For this reason WISE finds itself in a pioneering position, either working on issues, or concentrating on elements within issues, which many others are unable to reach.

For the "Vision" project, WISE invited a team of four people from the Third World to give their view of the state of the environment in the Netherlands and to critically assess the policies of the Dutch government and NGOs on sustainable development. We also asked them to give their vision of how the Netherlands, as an example to other industrialized countries, might change its direction in order to become sustainable. This report is the result of the team's work – which involved six weeks in October/November 1991 of literature study and interviews with organizations and individuals at all levels of Dutch society.

The four authors of this report are:

Mercio Gomes: Undersecretary of state for culture for the State of Rio de Janeiro, Brazil. Mercio has written a book called

"The Indians and Brazil" (in Portuguese) and has, as a cultural anthropologist, researched different Indian groups in the Amazon. He is also Professor of Cultural Anthropology at the University of Campinas, São Paulo and is chair of an organization which focuses on the political and cultural changes taking place in Brazilian society.

Chandra Kirana: Director of the Environmental Studies Project, an environmental organization based in Solo, Indonesia. Chandra has published for many years on a broad range of environmental themes.

Sami Songanbele: An agronomist from Tanzania, working with the Kilombero sugar company. Sami has experience in the areas of agriculture, irrigation and education and has a deep understanding of the erosion and forestry problems in her region. She also works in a women's organization which focuses on the education of rural women.

Rajiv Vora: An Indian Sociologist working as a researcher at the Gandhi Peace Foundation in New Delhi. Born in North West India (Gujarat), Rajiv has strong links with the grassroots movements in his country.

During their six weeks in the Netherlands, Mercio, Chandra, Sami and Rajiv carried out more than twenty interviews, talking with more than forty people representing industry, universities, government ministries, church organizations, peace organizations, environment organizations and development organizations. They travelled the length and breadth of the country by train, bus, taxi, boat and bicycle meeting farmers, theologians, academics, intellectuals, policy makers from government and industry, and environment and development activists. They also read, between them, hundreds of pages of reports, journals, books and articles as part of their work.

Within two weeks of meeting each other, the team had produced a synopsis and had divided the work into the seven sections which make up this book. The authors of the respective chapters are marked on the contents page.

As one reads through this book, one finds that the different chapters reflect the different social and cultural backgrounds of the team. Despite this, Mercio, Chandra, Sami and Rajiv are able to share a common view – a common experience – of the domination of their countries by the Northern culture.

The result of their hard work – this book – is an important companion not only to the National Report to the UNCED from the Netherlands, but also to the National Reports from other Northern countries.

Ian Tellam
Coordinator of the "Vision" project

Acknowledgements

We would like to acknowledge the help of the following people, without whose assistance the writing of this book could not have been possible.

Willy M. Douma, Stef M.H. Meijs, J.H.M. Pieters, J.A. Suurland – Ministry of Housing, Physical Planning and Environmental Management
Gerd Junne, Peter Konijn, Ans Kolk – Department of International Relations and Public International Law, University of Amsterdam
H. van der Kooi – Ministry of Agriculture, Nature Management and Fisheries
H.J.A. Schuurmans, Jope Cramwinkel – Environmental Policy Department, Shell Netherlands
Sible Schöne, Teo Wams, Paul van Sandbeek, Gerard Brinkman – Friends of the Earth (Milieudefensie), Netherlands
Jan Henselmans – Foundation for Nature and Environment (Natuur & Milieu)
Jan Juffermans and Jol Moors – The Small Earth (De Kleine Aarde)
Bram van Ojik – Novib
Heerko Dijksterhuis, Genevieve Eyck – Foundation for a New International Economic Order (NIO)
Pieter Lammers – Directorate General of International Foreign Affairs, Ministry of Foreign Affairs
Henk van Arkel – Aktie Strohalm
Andrea Berghuizen, Gerritt Vledder – Alliance for Sustainable Development
D.C. Mulder – Dutch Council of Churches

Marietje Kranendonk – National Environment Forum (Landelijk Milieu Overleg)
Joyce Kortland – Hunger Is Not Neccessary (Honger Hoeft Niet)
Coen van Beuningen – HIVOS
Vera Kappers – Pesticide Action Network
Petra Vervoort – CEBEMO
Rob Witte – CON
Edit Tuboly – Both ENDS
Maurits Groen – Freelance environmental journalist, Amsterdam
Jan Kuyper – Ecomare Ecological Centre, Texel
Ruud Gort – Freelance photographer, Amsterdam
Banawar – resident editor "Jansatta", New Delhi
Marja Tummers – Ecotec Resource BV
Joep Boer – Director, World Music Section, Rotterdam Conservatorium
Piet Dijkstra – Peace and development educationalist, Berghen
Professor Midden – Technical University Eindhoven
G. van Vendel, Stefan van Ede – Farm-owners near Wageningen
Mieke van der Zypp – University of Wageningen
Ronald Boon, Cristina Pannochia, Karen Kraakman, Marissa Irwin, Hermine Linnebank – WISE-Amsterdam
All the participants of the "Balancing the Future" NGO conference on environment and development, Zandvoort, November 1991
Everyone at the Rosenstock-Huessy House in Haarlem

Introduction

A well-known anthropological anecdote runs like this: if you stay a week in a different culture you might be able to understand it to the point of daring to write an article about it; if you stay a year or so you could eventually write a book; but if you should stay for a longer time and really live out that culture you would end up casting out your writings and admitting that you know very little of it. The anecdote was made up originally to express the difficulties in understanding Japanese culture but it can actually be extended to any culture in the world, including no doubt Dutch culture and society.

So, for the time we were given, the task we undertook with the utmost interest and care is now presented, not as a thesis on how the Dutch see their environment or *milieu,* or on what they should be trying to do to make things better and the world safer for everyone, but as a report: a condensed study on what we saw, on what we read, on what we heard casually said or calculatedly expressed about the state of the environment in the Netherlands and in its relation to the rest of the world.

This report has taken the opinions and the positions of many people in the Netherlands into consideration. In the first place, those of men and women who might be considered to be politically represented in governmental reports, such as *Concern for Tomorrow,* the National Environmental Report for UNCED 92, the Ministry of Development Cooperation book *A World of Differences,* and several others, plus signed articles and leaflets that are published by the ministries of Foreign Affairs, Development Cooperation, and Housing, Physical Planning and the Environment. In other words, the State's point of view. Secondly, the views of the *environment* militants as expressed in books, reports, leaflets, brochures, working papers and the like presented by Dutch NGOs criticizing governmental reports and/or giving their own viewpoints on environmental issues. Thirdly, there were the general talks, interviews, and workshops with NGO militants, governmental officials, one or two politicians, an important clergyman, journalists with expertise on environmental and political issues, and, last but not least, with so many randomly selected Dutch people – especially the members of the Rosenstock Huessey House, in Haarlem, whom we want to thank for the warm hospitality. Finally, we might consider the bits and pieces of observation of curious or common things spotted in the streets, supermarkets, department stores, free markets, bars, a few home visits – things that sometimes give a clue to understanding certain attitudes, or threads with which one can sew the loose ends and join the pieces of fabric that, put together, constitute the irregular patterns of a culture.

Although black and brown, four different pairs of eyes from three different continents and fairly different backgrounds looked into the subject of Dutch environment. Some common grounds were immediately found, not just by oppositon or negation to the subject investigated but from sociocultural experiences that appeared very similar and which showed themselves in common attitudes and perhaps common viewpoints. The least significant of which was not a certain propensity for laughing, for joking around, for talking aimlessly, for being near or touching or holding one another by the hand, by the arm or around the shoulders in signs of closeness and friendship.

What, after all, could a Ghandian Hindu sociologist who thinks the *chakra* is India's future have in common with a Brazilian anthropologist who, notwithstanding his working conviction that the Brazilian Indios will survive, thinks the way to go is onwards? Or how could a Tanzanian agronomist who works wholeheartedly in a para-state sugar mill find a close identity with an Indonesian psychologist determined to encumber some of her own country's development projects? Or, worse, how could such traditionally rivalrous religious backgrounds as Islamism, Hinduism, and Christian Catholicism, practiced in higher or lesser degrees as each culture goes, come to terms on moral and philosophical grounds? Well, believe it or not, we did.

There is, to begin with, a shared if perhaps not always clearly defined feeling that the world has that mysterious quality of being one and at the same time being many, of being single and diverse, of having one goal but many ways to get to it. So our diversities are understood as part of the nature of things and represent only variations on the same theme. This characteristic is what allows for a certain feeling of tolerance, on the one hand, and the wish to know of the other's ways, on the other, if only to make fun of it. It is a trait, so to speak, common to all cultures but it only gets developed when the need for cooperation surpasses the drive for competition. It is not, however, a dominant trait, for the ethnocentrism that is its negation maintains itself ready to surface when necessary. All the same, when developed, this characteristic makes oneself more open to the world, more willing to accept differences and therefore more apt to understand others. Including, of course, whoever may be on top.

From this feeling for diversity another possible shared trait emerged, which is the idea that there are other ways, as there were so many in the past, which can be conceived as alternatives for the development of our societies and per chance for the future of mankind as a whole. Perhaps this idea did not exist clearly in each one of our minds, but it certainly forced its way out when our discussions about the old and the proposedly new relations between environment and development heated up.

What could be those general alternative ways, we dared not fathom yet, but for each country, for each one of the some 170 countries in the world as many alternatives could arise provided there were workable political and economic conditions and a new outlook into the cooperative possibilities of mankind based on firm principles of social justice and equity

The highly mechanized harbour industry, where Southern goods enter the Dutch market place. (Photo Ruud Gort)

among nations and a clear-cut commitment to nonviolence as a means to achieve those goals.

And here, thinking we might have worked out an easy solution ourselves – later we realized these principles had also been thought out by NGO activists, which suggests that our frames of reference were the same – we entered the discussion of what we look like, or rather, how are we perceived by the ruling powers of the world, the centre of Western civilization, or the "North", as it is calling itself now. We, by opposition, are called the "South". The picture that could be drawn, of course, would not be very pleasing to the eye, neither to theirs nor to ours. It certainly has never even looked proportionate to its real figure, but now it seems it is becoming worse than ever. We are indeed not only looking strange and pitiful, but especially objectionable if not disgusting, to the masters of power. Why is that?

Well, it takes more time to analyze this and come to a good conclusion than we could afford. But one clue we could pursue with less difficulty, and that was this new denomination we have received. Why are we now being called "Southerners", if that was not some bad-tasting innuendo spurted out by some American yankee against his ever mistrusted racist confederate compatriots? No, there was something else to this. It seems that this change of name had started in the mid-80s but it only became justifiable when the Berlin Wall crumbled to pieces and a new chance for Europe and the former called "First World" arose to enlarge its field of economic interest and its range of political power. Given the eagerness with which Eastern European countries were demonstrating their willingness to undertake the ways that have produced the superaffluent style of life of their Western neighbours, there should not be any difficulty in encompassing these countries into the fold of Western power centres. So they quickly lost their status of Second World and by a touch of linguistic magic became first worlders, or "Northerners". One could say indeed that all those countries are geographically in the northern hemisphere, as are the United States and Canada and even Japan, but never Australia and enclaved white South Africa.

Southerners, coloureds, non-whites, third worlders or whatever we may be called, it is not really important. But we felt it necessary to point out that the new name is not intentionally descriptive; it hides a political process which seems to be unfolding itself and whose aims are the growth of political power and the tightening of the domination of the present power centres over the peripheral areas. For the challenges that face this power centre – and the environment is just one, albeit more visible – require as much strength as possible, as much determination and surgery-like precision as possible, and as much subtle intelligence as can be summoned. Dividing the world in two seems to be a nice way to glue whatever countries you want in one of the halves, and leave the other to its own solutions. In this sense, then, the diversity of national interests and personal views that were present in all four of us found one more unifying common ground, this time imposed from the outside and with a new label.

Do we as "South" have the means to negotiate better terms in the relationship with the "North"? Is the environment issue an end in itself or is it part of a more complicated game where many other cards are not on the table? The answers to these questions seemed to be easy to grasp but all the same this was an opportunity to make a concerted effort in opening a new and frank dialogue with people who were themselves critical of their own world and who wanted to receive new inputs to help strengthen their own arguments. We were, in a sense, seeing the monster from the inside, but in the process we also exposed ourselves, this report being perhaps the most conspicuous act.

For all this, we wish to make it clear that the enterprise that we were invited to undertake was not guided by any bias against the West – for, alas, some of our countries are but offshoots of this civilization. We understand that there is multiplicity in any oneness and there has always been a small reasonable section within Western civilization that has not been guided by a sense of power over the world. Here we are

"No more chlorine" – Friends of the Earth (Milieudefensie) at AKZO
(Photo Ruud Gort)

guided by the best of our traditions: the trust and friendship
reposed in us by our Dutch friends could only be reciprocated
by being honest and truthful to them.

If a Southern view on the question of environment exists, it
is first of all that it cannot possibly be dissociated from the
problems generally referred to as development. Development
needs a new definition. Sustainablility also needs to be re-
defined or rather given a more precise definition, which takes
into account the whole process of international trade, political
power, and cultural and economic balancing. But what is really
meaningful to this view is that it should set apart the very
question of technical analysis and technical solutions, including economic calculations, from the core perception of the
environmental deadlock in which the whole world is living.

Ours therefore had to be a different approach, and it turned out to be fundamentally a philosophical analysis in that we perceived the whole environmental issue within the total context of culture, in the present case, Dutch life in European civilization.

Civilizational and cultural questions have to be asked now. They will be harsh and will challenge the very foundations supporting the whole apparatus and the whole maintenance structure of Western civilization. It is clear to all that, since power lies in this civilization, and unless it restricts its appetite, it shall go on impoverishing the entire earth. It is also proven by history that this civilization has the particular habit of cannibalizing non-white people. Thirdly, it has as yet done nothing to inspire trust amongst the so-called Third World countries. Fourthly, whenever opportunity showed, the Western powers have collectively said good-bye to fairplay and justice and have effectively demonstrated their arrogance from the field of trade to war and to peace.

A deeper analysis of our behaviour is necessary, not only of how we misbehave with each other as human beings, for we know why that is. But when we extend such behaviour beyond us, when our internal violence overreaches other segments of nature of which we ourselves are but a part, we need a deeper and radical rethinking about all that goes into the making of ourselves. The changes and rearrangements within the constitution of human society may go on at its various levels, including national and international levels; but if such changes require – of necessity – radical transformations of nature itself, then we must realize that we are stretching "our" world too far, and overpressing our little kingdom beyond its mandate.

Chapter 1

In search of sustainability

A first look into history

Next year it will be five hundred years since Columbus's discovery of America. And four years after that Vasco da Gama's journey around Africa and into the Indian Ocean. These are the symbols of Europe's drive for the conquest of the non-white world. After five hundred years they have gained dominance over others but that might prove to be temporary. The UNCED conference, which coincides with this important anniversary, provides an opportunity to us to dispassionately examine what has gone into building what is known as the modern Western civilization and to analyze its new holocaust image: the destruction of the earth itself.

We wish to understand the nature of the problem of the environment, not as if to present the views of the other half, the South, and thus unwittingly accept the inevitability of having north-south dichotomy, but we wish instead to contribute to creating a holistic understanding. The problem of the environment is neither an accidental phenomenon nor a marginal abberation of modern industrialization. The destruction of the balance within nature was inherent in the basic frame of mind which created modern industrialization of the Western type. We can properly understand environmental destruction only when we see it in relation to other types of destruction which have not yet become our prime concerns. That is the reason we must look into the historical process of the past five hundred years.

What started as Europe's journey into "civilized" life and prosperity required large-scale annihilation and the slave trade. About 112 million native Americans were annihilated and close to twenty million Africans were brought as slaves from Central and Western Africa to America, while millions of Africans suffered the same inhuman violence at the hands of Europeans. That is how the Americas were built to be what they are today.

In Asia, human slaughtering was also carried out massively, but not to the point of razing its populations to minimal levels. Europe succeeded in destroying only the institutional fabric of Asian and African societies by transforming their political systems according to the European mould and simultaneously de-industrializing them. Initially this was done through political subjugation, but later modern education itself became instrumental in this process; even in those countries which were not politically subjugated.

In the course of this historical process, the European image of man has undergone a drastic change. He became devoid of divinity, lost his love for nature and became rebellious towards all social relations. As a result he became an atomized individual, separated from God, Nature and Society. This atomized psyche has been glorified all these centuries as the "free man" who enjoys his freedom through market choice and what is termed as "democracy" of the Western type.

Science and destruction

The creation of a power that is legitimized by the conquest of others depends on the usurpation of the autonomy of man on the one hand, and, on the other, the destruction of life through the medium of science and technology of the modern type. The pronounced goal of modern science is to conquer nature.[1] It is now realized that nature is beyond man, because man is just a part of it, and it therefore cannot be conquered by him. However, modern science has been interfering with natural processes to create heightened energy for our use, and has been continuously destroying life to create an artificial mass. In other words, the modern affluence of the North is the result of converting animate world into something inanimate. It was only logical for modern science and technology to create the nuclear bomb and its arsenal. In order to a nuclear bomb to explode, an atom is split to offset the natural balance between centrifugal and centripetal forces, thus releasing centrifugal energy at its most explosive speed. Not much reflection is required to understand that the whole body of modern science and technology is an activated slow motion nuclear bomb, as it does not respect natural processes and destroys life. Its destructive implications have to date been seen only in the form of environmental degradation. We will have to take a holistic view of creation to be able to comprehend fully the multifaceted destructive power of modern western science and technology and its consequences. We are suffering the consequences. We are unaware of their cause, however.

Like the Bhasmasura of Indian mythology, who had the gift to turning to ashes anyone on whose head he put his hand, Europe has wrought destruction wherever it laid its hands. The Bhasmasura finally extended his hand toward lord Shiva, who had given him the gift, but the lord Vishnu enchanted him in such a way that he unwittingly put his hand on his own head and brought on his own self-destruction.

Are not the facts about poisoning of the soil, air and water in the Netherlands sufficient to show the Dutch people – in fact the Northern people – that you have put your hand on that which has given you the gift of your life?

The impact of the Western system on the world

The present situation of multiple degradation – each sustaining the other – is the creation of colonial plunder and the subsequent transformation of everyone's political, economic and cultural systems and moral basis. This transformation created not only alien and artificial power structures in Southern societies but also created in their minds doubt as to the worth of their traditional thought, history, collective talent and capacities. There was no design in this because Europeans genuinely thought that their own system was modern and universal and therefore wanted colonized people to conform to their standards. The emergence of this world system, as we have explained, has produced slavish tendencies within its own societies. It was obvious therefore that the modern European rule would cripple non-European societies and convert them into servile and slavish societies.

There is now enough historical material to conclude that before European conquest American, African and Asian societies had attained a state of cultural maturity and prosperity without disturbing the balance within nature. African and American civilization were no inferior to the European civilization of that time. Civilizations like those of India and China the Mayas and the Incas, and the Muslim World, were vibrant and prosperous in their philosophical thinking, political structures, science and technology.

The Indian example

We can take 18th century India as an example which shows amply that the level of material well-being was of high order. Its political system was based on the autonomy of its communicatian units in the areas of political and juridical administration. The economic system was based on the principle of local self-sufficiency in food, housing, clothing, health, education, and a number of cultural functions which enriched social life. Common property rights were vested in supremacy of the authority of the community closest to its resources so that there was a sense of strong collective belongingness and collective responsibility. These are the most primary conditions for non-exploitative, reciprocal relationships with the environment and within the society. Science and technology provided a high degree of productivity without damaging natural processes and the capacity to provide effective answers to the challenges of both internal and external relations.

Modern academics have portrayed India and other societies

as being stagnant. On the basis of this image Karl Marx legitimized the colonial rule and hoped that it would lead to progress. But no serious scholar would believe today, for example, that India was a stagnant society. The myth has been exploded. The facts are that even after Muslim rule, about 25% of the Indian population was engaged in industry around AD 1800. India was producing superior steel to Europe and the total production of steel compared favourably with the total production of steel in the whole of Europe at that time. Indian agricultural technology, based only on organic methods, was very advanced and sophisticated, and Indian farmers were using the drill plough, for example, for the last 1000 years or more, whereas it was introduced in Europe only in the nineteenth century. The productivity of agriculture was so high that even in the less fertile district of Chingelpet in the south of India 120 tons of rice was an average per hectare at that time. The five hundred thousand villages of India had one school each and literacy among Indian peasants was rated by British rulers in the first half of the 19th century as amazingly the highest in the world. Each village had at least one ayurvedic doctor. And finally there was a self governing council for the general administration of village and local affairs.

Moreover, the nature of Indian society was egalitarian. There does not seem to be much unjust disparity among various social segments in terms of consumption of food and general consumer goods for a simple and healthy life. For example, quoting Thomas Munro, Dharampal, a renounced scholar of 18th century India, provides us with the facts about the real consumption and nutritional intake of the three social classes into which Munro classified Indian people. While fuel-wood consumption of a family of six persons in the first class amounted to Rupees 7-4-8 pa., in the second class it was Rs 3-10-0 pa. and in the third class Rs 2-11-0 pa. The poorest and the richest ate similar food in terms of usual items of basic nutritional value, like grains, pulses, oil, ghee (butter), milk, and fresh vegetables. Nutritional intake and energy consumption of the lowest category family of 18th century India would compare very well with the similar consumption by the modern middle classes. The poor of the present times is a newly developed economic class – a direct result of Western "progress and development". They were never poor historically when they were masters of their affairs. Development debates and theories are based on historically false premises on this account. In this light, it is an insult to these people to propagate that population growth in the South is the reason for poverty. Moreover, it does not help us locate the real cause.

The main characteristics of traditional Indian civilization are moral order, plural authority, institutional interdependence, autonomous communities and nature oriented science and technology. The colonial rule destroyed or crippled this order piece by piece. The moral order was replaced by hierarchy and centralized power, the moral life style was converted into a hedonistic economic life. Authority was totally centralized and its plural nature was destroyed in the name of establishing a Western rule of law. All the institutions were brought into subservience to the state and thus their interdependence and reciprocal mutual functions, responsibility and power were subverted and usurped. The autonomy of communities was totally disregarded and they were made servile to external power. With the collapse of this supportive system, nature oriented science and technology became resourceless. At the same time colonial powers used a highly exploitative – almost plunderous – revenue mechanism to cripple Indian industry and to transform Indian agriculture so as to create surplus for the empire-building and for its urban elite, by forcing peasantry to adopt monoculture farming.

This resulted in disorientation of mind, disruption of social and political life, pauperization of the economy of the common Indians, degradation of nature. Common Indians found themselves disabled in the performance of their rightful duty.

In the midst of this century India regained its political freedom. It accelerated its production by improving the a better organization of modern political, economic, scientific and technological systems. Achievements of economic growth are by all means quite impressive. India has produced more modern consumers and consumer products than many of the industrially advanced countries. Yet India looks poor and restless. The reason lies in its disorientation. The growth is mechanical and based on the creation of internal colonization in its society. It breeds poverty by over-utilising the resources of the whole society for the benefit of a small modernized section. This growth does not benefit common Indian people and their institutions.

Neocolonization and its new results

In the latter half of this century the political colonization came to an end, and subjugated societies became free nations. The fight against disabilities created during the colonial period was their national priority. The situation was almost paralysingly difficult as they found themselves in a grossly unequal world in which one part had become highly rich and powerful. They started emulating the Western nations, thinking that by doing so they would be able to stand with them as equals. This has finally proved otherwise, even fatal. The alternative would have been to draw the necessary confidence from their tradition. But the new ruling class of these newly freed nations was totally severed from its roots, intellectually and culturally. It was created by the colonial powers as their comprador class.

The North knew what it was doing. Its strategy in facing this new situation was to promote development in order to incorporate the rest of the world in its economic system.

The strategy of global development has accelerated the crisis of our time. As the Brundtland Report says, "Industrial production has grown more than fifty-fold over the past century, four-fifths of this growth since 1950". This may be seen within the context of energy depletion that it has required. The increase in consumption of fossil fuels for example is a good indicator. Half of the world's production of coal has occurred only since 1930 and half of its oil consumption only since 1952. Among various mineral fuels, petroleum accounts for nearly three-fourths of the world's production by value. This is just to illustrate what this four-fifths of fifty-fold growth of industrialism since 1950 means – its resource destructibility.

How many people have benefitted from this fifty-fold increase in industrial production, of which four-fifths has occurred only between 1950 and 1990? Perhaps no more than one fifth of the world population. The conclusion does not need much data and analysis, it is unambiguous. Modern industrialism, which has exhausted more than half of its total source of life within just less than half a century in the process of enabling only a tiny but powerful section of the world's population to reap its fruits, could not be sustainable, much less has it any capacity or even tendency to propel itself towards equity and moral order.

Consider the implications of the fact that the energy base which was thought to be infinite, and upon which the entire edifice of a new and modern so-called global civilization is constructed, is extremely finite. The claims of the modern society are falsified. Not only the edifice but the very core of its claims seem to be heading towards disintegration – even to its avowed protagonists. Therefore the problem faced by both the "developed" countries and their so called "progressive" counterparts is as to how to prolong the period of their lifestyle and power. The future of their power and indulgence is threatened.

Crisis of survival is an inner problem of the industrialized "developed" societies. Instead of seriously reflecting on the very nature of this inner crisis of modern Western industrialism, it seems that people in the North are trying to wish it away – ostrich like – through symbolism of demonstrative antics.[2]

However the purpose of "developing" the South is to make it a part of the Western destiny, as it is already in its political fold; the central principle of modern industrial civilization is a slave-society the need for whose resources it can devour. It turns the resources into a consumable mass. The crisis of resources is thus the direct consequence of the central tendencies of modern lifestyle – stealing, hoarding and waste[3].

Every Dutch person produces as much waste as a small business in the Third World. (Photo Jos van der Hamsvoord/HH)

These tendencies have become satiated even by "development". Through development the North and its support systems in the South have further de-industrialized large and remaining parts of Asia, Africa and Latin America. This has facilitated what was achieved during colonial days through an extremely taxing revenue system and the drainage of wealth and resources from the less developed towards those already developed regions. Many a self-sufficient society thus became buyers of Northern goods, technologies and training. In the course of development, they acquired the unbearable burden of debt which has locked them into a vicious cycle of development, debt, and drainage. This has been made possible by, among other things, creating an increasingly higher geographic and political distance between the consumer and the producer. And now even environmental thought and action plans are produced as a package in places increasingly inaccessible to their Southern "consumers".

Development theories, and hence strategies, are based on Western theory of historical evolution. One of the very important documents of the Dutch government, *A World of Difference* notes: "India, which has made considerable macroeconomic progress in the past 40 years, has a population of 800 million, some 500 million of whom have derived little or no benefit from this 'progress'." The writer of this document should be aware of the fact that many of these 500 million are those who were de-industrialised, de-stabilised and exploited in order that the so-called macro-economic progress became possible. The report further notes: "In Latin America the economic crisis means struggle for existence and survival for very many..." (p.36) This is explained away in the report as "structural dualism". The report accepts the fact that there is a link between structural dualism in the world economy and structural dualism in the economies of both the developing and the industrialized countries. It further notes that "it has recently been strengthened by the increasingly transnational nature of decision on production, trade and investments. The world economy is no more a sum of national markets; it is itself a 'world market, with fewer and fewer partitions between sectors, since transnational enterprises have developed into conglomerates, operating in many sectors simultaneously'..." The crux of the issue is that the gap between those who have sufficient access to factors which determine economic modernization and those with very limited access is becoming increasingly unsurmountable." (p.36)

Sound and unsound basis of sustainable development

European theorization and interpretation of historical evolution, which was essentially a European experience, was universalized through power and colonial education. The essential aspect of this theorization is its interpretation of what they call the historical evolution of "mankind". Human life is explained as having passed through various stages in an "evolutionary" order, finally arriving to the "enlightened" stage of the industrial age. Continuing in this theory, only the modern Western life is believed to be the most "evolved", "progressive", "developed" form of life. Consequently all other cultures are pre-historic and backward. However, if harmony with nature, peaceful co-existence between species and human groups, simplicity, non-violence, justice and equity, and superior moral and ethical values guided by non-violent and non-exploitative urgency are our yard-sticks for measuring progress and development, than there is not even one iota of evidence to suggest that the modern industrial way of life is in any way superior to a number of non-Western ways of life, *i.e.* tribal, peasant, agro-pastoral.

Once this theory of historical evolution is accepted the rest of the disciplines of the modern knowledge system follow. The modern knowledge system is created in the service of the industrial society. It is highly doubtful whether sustainable development with global equity and justice can be achieved through the Western knowledge system and its general attitude of imperial relationship with other knowledge systems.

The truest and, if there is one, shortest road to sustainability lies in the recognition of other cultural lifestyles, their knowledge systems, their sovereign sense of destiny and finally and primarily in their empowerment.

The internal crisis of modern industrialism and development is forcing people to looking for better alternatives and, at the same time, to listen to environmentalists and other radical groups. Thus development is now being qualified by the concept of sustainability. The definition of sustainable development varies from environmental modernism to austere materialism. Both of these approaches to sustainability fall short of what is in reality required. For they do not correct the perception of man and the world and do not reform scientific and technological outlooks. Without reforms of this order, sustainability will always remain in conflict with development; and this conflict will remain unresolved.

The Brundtland Commission's definition of sustainable development – which is, with rare exception[4], lapped up by almost all – stands, in the light of the above, as a guarantee against any serious change in outlook, international relationships, market structures or public policies. It is open ended, for it does not take any inspiration from the past. It is sterile, because, in spite of its desire, vividly expressed, it is intrinsically incapable of delivering resource-equity and therefore environmental stability. It does not provide any instruments for reducing the resource claims of the North over the South. However, it advocates, promotes and promises environmental modernization; *i.e.* modernization with the environment as its excuse. The North may produce an environmentally efficient car for

A typical Dutch freeway scene. (Photo Michiel Wijnbergh/HH)

the Dutch, for example. But if in a huge' environmentally friendly car only one person is to travel – or at the most two, and every family is going to have a car or two; who is more environmentally friendly: such a European; or Asians, African and Latin Americans who use cars, buses and trains to their full capacity? And how many of them own a car!

At the end of a technological process is the society and its people. If it is not possible to produce energy efficient individuals, technologies will not succeed.

Every step towards modernization – whatever the excuse – will invariably push Southern societies towards debt, poverty and instability. Therefore modernization should be real cultural modernization in terms of:

a. awareness of the existing global cultural resources which can provide the understanding necessary to reshape this wasteful and anti-nature industrial system and its equally wasteful and inefficient market system into a nature conserving industrialism and efficient and responsible market system; and

b. cultural re-discovery of Southern societies and their de-Westernization.

Only through culturally authentic rule can Third World countries create their countervailing power, for power resides chiefly in cultural authenticity. Without that only the modern industrial way of life will continue to be reinforced. *The entire debate on sustainability and development is silent on this fundamental issue.*

Take for example the very question of environment raised within the development debate. It would be revealing if someone were to conduct research to examine the impact of the so-called "environmental awareness" campaigns conducted in many of the Third World countries. So many reports have shown that many communities in which the relationship with the environment was organic and therefore reciprocal have been further alienated from their common property rights over environmental resources, which traditionally belonged to them. The "developed" ruling class of the North became the

final custodians and ultimate arbitrator in the course of arous-
ing environmental awareness. Even to the extent that the USA's
"arbitration" in the name of peace and human rights in the
Middle East was essentially an act of establishing itself and the
North as the final custodians of the Gulf oil resources.

Thus silence on some of the most fundamentally crucial
questions needs to be broken in order to understand sustainability in relation to power positions.

Let us take for example the category "standard of living"[6],
the anvil upon which everything is tested and the altar at which
sacrifices on the part of the masses of the Third World are
invited and sanctified. When we talk of "standard of living",
particularly when it means that the modern way of life is the
"standard", the category "standard of life" becomes the most
central function of power. What is known as "progress" and
"development" has no intrinsic motivity. It has no motive
force of its own. Power has been its motive force. It is the force
of power which has propelled it and keeps it going. Unless,
therefore, the relationship between power and progress and
progress and poverty are impartially exposed, along with the
nature of that power behind them, all exercises remain integral
to commitment to the modern Western way of life in spite of
our otherwise good intentions and emotional responses.

If we wish to be honest and truthful, we shall have to reject
many such concepts to discover or rediscover our own categories of interpretation. Only then will our minds become
free from the falsehood of developmentalist doctrine, the falsehood regarding the modern life style and its intellectual, technological and institutional infrastructure. The prevailing doctrine of development, including that of sustainable development, inhibits a truthful interpretation of the poverty, environmental crisis, and affluence, by maintaining silence on the
crucial question of power. And therefore, in the essential sense,
that is a secret doctrine.

In addition, this doctrine is based on a world view which
regards the affluence of some as intrinsically unrelated to the
poverty and pauperization of the others. At the same time it

rejects all cultures other than the modern Western one and propounds that the destiny of all societies the world over is to become part of the Western system and thus part of the destiny of the North. It is for that reason that Northern people see their own life as the standard yardstick, even for others. We must decipher the intrinsic relationship between affluence of the one section of the global society and the pauperization of the other.

The modern world-view inhibits a truthful interpretation of reality by isolating only certain aspects of life as areas of degradation while at the same time it declares certain other areas as vibrantly healthy and progressive. For example, the Brundtland Report notes: "... on the development side, in terms of absolute numbers there are more hungry people in the world than ever before, and their numbers are increasing. So are the numbers who cannot read or write, the numbers without safe water or safe and sound homes, and the numbers short of woodfuel with which to cook and warm themselves. The gap between rich and poor nations is widening – not shrinking – and there is little prospect, given present trends and institutional arrangements, that this process will be reversed."[7] While at the same time it notes "... Fortunately, this new reality coincides with more positive developments new to this century. We can move information and goods faster around the globe than ever before; we can produce more food and more goods with less investment of resources; our technology and science gives us at least the potential to look deeper into and better understand natural systems. From space, we can see and study the Earth as an organism whose health depends on the health of all its parts. We have the power to reconcile human affairs with natural laws and to thrive in the process. In this our cultural and spiritual heritages can reinforce our economic interests and survival imperatives."[8]

Let us analyze this double talk. The fundamental premise upon which endeavours are conducted is that the world is one. Yes, that is the dominant reality. But it is not one just because one can easily travel from one end to the other. Philius Phog had done it long ago in 80 days, when the world was not one.

It is one because all the forms of organization of human life and culture – civilizations – are in a process of merging their identities into the image and organization of the Northern industrial civilization. It is a global system within which all nations function, and become "one". We must, within this context, understand that the health of a body, of a system, which is organically one, never decays in some parts while it simultaneously gains in other of its parts. This applies both to the individual and to the global society. If certain parts of the society, global or national, seem to be gaining strength and vitality while other parts decay, this should be recognised as the case of a parasitic relationship between them.

Similarly, the very title of the Brundtland Report, *Our Common Future,* is double talk. How can Southern peoples be now persuaded that they share a common future with the North if they did not share a common past nor are being invited to share the present – unless one completely twists the real meaning of sharing.

If for instance the Dutch people are able to put to their use some other nations' lands – as the figures go, three times more than their own land – and if the inhabitants of those lands have not become, in the course of serving Dutch people, as prosperous as the Dutch farmers who also serve Dutch people with their land, then the relationship with these other people cannot but be called parasitic and never could it be understood as sharing. For, if they were to use similarly any portion of the land of any of the "developed" nations, the tillers of that land would be reaping the same benefits as their Dutch counterparts.

The North needs to be receptive and fearless

As the question of power is central to the understanding of the relationship between modern Western lifestyle and environmental disaster, we need also look into the cultural and moral aspects of this relationship. Culture shapes people's ideas about moral and immoral conduct and in turn culture itself gets further influenced by them. It is a dynamic process. This in turn shapes the nature of politics and political power and social practices.

As a matter of fact the North has been too present-minded and considers its own world view as the best suited for the whole world. This has resulted in an extremely partial interpretation of the environmental crisis. The North wants to resolve the crisis without a radical transformation of its thought, structures and development processes. Largely because of the fear of loss of the prosperity it has achieved in the post world war two era, it does not understand the possibility that a certain reduction in this kind of prosperity might increase the quality of their life. A continuous dependence on this "modern" way of life is also due to a lack of any historical experience of cultural and material prosperity through other ways of life as well as a certain ignorance about working out alternative ways. In a strong sense the North is in a state of cultural helplessness. This stems from the fact that the North has ceased to be receptive towards other cultures, as it initially was as it needed to adopt ideas and institutions of other cultures to meet their internal and external challenges. Receptivity presupposes selfless and meaningful enquiry. The North's arrogance about the self, a trait so characteristic of nouveau riche behaviour and of those to whom power comes undeservedly, accounts for its closed-mindedness.

As power raised Europe and then the United States – the North – to dominance, its receptivity receded and it started to massify the world in order to secure a world-wide market. Thus it perpetuated its dominance. Its power infatuation is such that it hardly realizes that this dominance can prove to be a temporary phenomenon. It is in the nature of power that it goes on shifting its centre. If tiny Japan can compel huge Soviet Russia to change its political and economic system, there is no guarantee that a new power would not ever emerge to compel the market empire of the North to re-shape itself radically.

We should keep in mind that this market empire is built upon grossly wasteful structures which make it increasingly less efficient[9]. But its inefficiency is concealed by its transnational economic imperialism.

Finding sustainability

The problem of perception notwithstanding, the environment and sustainability debate has achieved an historic success. The success lies in the new understanding of the nature of the North.[10] Until now the church as well as the enlightenment literature taught people that nature was the preserve of man. Western science went a step ahead and proclaimed nature to be an enemy of man and therefore set as its aim and those of technology to conquer it. It is the environmental crisis which has now forced the North to look at other cultures of Latin America, Africa and Asia which have lived in harmony with nature. For the first time in its history the North has come to realize that nature is all pervasive and man is but a part of it. Thus it has now become blasphemous to think that man can be master of nature. Man, endowed with innovative mind and skills, can overcome certain vagaries of nature, as the Dutch have done with particular regard to sea, but it must be realized that he can do this within the permissible limits and laws of nature.

This realization has removed a serious obstacle in the thought of Northern and Western oriented people. But it has not yet solved the problem because no convincing alternatives to market production and its supporting systems is in sight. It is here that a new breakthrough is required. And in order to achieve this breakthrough we shall have to correct our image of man.

If man is estimated as an economic animal we shall not be able to see him as anything other than a blind consumer engaged in endless consumption – a consummate devourer of nature. This consumer image of man is only a transplantation of an earlier image of slave who was thought to be devoid of moral judgement. In the same vein the modern consumer has no moral limits to his consumption.

It should be realized that man can only seek the attainment of his true nature. This consists in a plurality of dispositions that balance each other out. Man is disposed towards truth, non-violence, valour, material well being and innovative skills. A good and developed society provides every opportunity for the development of these dispositions. Northern society has undermined truth, non-violence, valour and innovativeness. Only a few are supposed to acquire these qualities and the rest of the society is seen as passive participants.

They "participate" by way only of providing conditions for a few to attain non-materialist goals or by simply indulging in endless consumption which is bribed to them so as to maintain them morally inactive. Now, if we desire to maximize this bribe there is no better way than the modern industrialization which keeps society either as a help to mechanical processes and/or as a mere participant in mechanical consumption – all regulated by the market process.

However, the material well-being of all is a necessary goal which we should try to attain. This goal can be best achieved when there is no conflict between man and man nor between man and nature. It is here that we realize the principle of equity and the principle of sustainability. These principles can be economically organized in the manner of a model system like that known as the Indian "swadeshi" principle. This principle was actively followed in its multiple implication in India and more or less according to the needs of their societies in Asia, Africa and Latin America.

In essence this principle implies "the use and service of the closest to the exclusion of the farther". But this applies not only to the field of economic needs but equally to one's political, cultural and spiritual needs. By this principle we can provide an operational guideline and an operational model of sustainable development which will range from local to global levels. It should be noted here that there always was an international market, and distant societies (for example North China and Western Europe used to trade with each other. But this trade was restricted to exotic things, or to things which had a natural surplus production like spices. To trade with natural surplus is one thing and to create surplus by monoculture an convert every region into economic colony of market forces totally another thing[II].

For a long time in history this sustainability principle has remained operative in all the traditional societies including those in Europe. Indeed, only in short periods of Western history, like the Roman period and the present, has greed for power made the ruling classes so blind and foolish as to disregard this principle. This is the time we must recapture the wisdom of old, and turn the destiny of mankind towards its normal healthy course in history.

Notes

1   "On a small square in the city of Rotterdam – one of the world's biggest ports and a major industrial centre – is a plaque which informs the reader that were it not for the dykes, he or she would be approximately seven metres below sea-level.

These are perhaps a few things that typify the Netherlands so well: on the one hand, all the hustle and bustle of a major industrial and commercial city and, on the other hand, the sobering thought that it all would be destroyed if man was not longer able to control nature." This is the opening paragraph of the Netherlands National Report to UNCED, page 5.

2   In the energy crisis: "energy efficient cook stoves" and biogas for the poor countries, energy efficient motor cars in the USA and steel factories in Japan, or recycling of beer-cans in Europe (For a detailed advocacy of this path to salvation see the "State of the World" Reports, 1984-91, Worldwatch Institute, USA.

3   Waste is a Dutch national problem – but more than the very great visible waste there is a lot more which is invisible, the major being the waste of energy in modern production and market system. High level consumption of meat, and fertilizer-pesticide, is the other kind of invisible waste.

4   Thijs de la Court, "Beyond Brundtland"

5 "Americans drive 'huge' cars, not us!", quote from a Dutch friend.

6 Rajiv Vora in "Prashna Paryavaran no?" (Gujarati) Hind Swaraj Mandal, Rajkot, Gujarat, India, 1989.

7 *Our Common Future,* World Commission on Environment and Development, 1987, p.2

8 ibid. p.1

9 Both the problems of the Netherlands, that of dung and waste, are the best examples. But their wastefulness is not recognised as being intrinsic to the economic structure, mainly due to the transnational nature of the meat business.

10 See for example:

   I NGO's report to the UNCED, Dutch Alliance for Sustainable Development, 1991

   II Netherlands Environmental Policy Plan

   III *A World of Difference* published by the Dutch Ministry of Development Cooperation, 1991 (one of the most important documents from this point of view.

11 "One effect of growing economic integration is that more and more natural products are transported over ever greater distances, thus increasingly disrupting ecological cycles. A well known example is the tapioca imported into the Netherlands from Thailand for use as fodder. This results in the loss of soil fertility in Thailand and excessive manuring in the Netherlands." from *A World of Difference,* Dutch Ministry of Development Cooperation, 1991, p.81

Chemical waste to be burned. (Photo Michiel Wijnbergh/HH)

Chapter 2

Dutch environment as they see it

Pollution is a relatively recent phenomenon in the cultural experiences of most peoples and is felt in many different ways. As a physical reality pollution has of course existed for quite some time, in the North at least since industrialization, but it was conceptualized only as a marginal phenomenon. Nevertheless it was the growing awareness of pollution that caused the perception of environment as a reality apart from the concept of nature and as a problem. This began in a simple and direct way by seeing the accumulating amounts of trash on the streets, bicycles in the canals, smog in the air, fetid smells in the countryside, waste dumps, and the like. These sense perceptions touch people in an immediate way and leave no doubt in anyone's mind about what is pollution. But they are a sort of continuation of previous experiences that seem to have intensified in a higher ratio than one can expect from a few years back. People can recall that as children or young adults a lot of other dirty things were easily seen in bigger amounts than now. So it appears to be only a matter of intensification of certain polluting practices or a change in the materials that cause this bad sight.

The usual response to that is that something can be done about it, if only government were more responsable, or people changed their habits and got better educated in relation to what they should do in public. For anyone can see that privately most people take good care of their own belongings and their houses are usually kept impeccably tidy and clean.

This kind of sense perception of pollution seems to be quite natural and can be found in any country in the world, for two main reasons. First because, as was said above, it just appears as a continuation of former life experiences and in some senses it represents a kind of price that one can pay for the improvement in one's life style. This is particularly obvious in relation to the use of cars. Secondly, and most importantly, because most countries constitute themselves in unegalitarian societies with loose feelings for communitarian livelihood and social responsability. In these societies usually a strong clear-cut distinction is made between what is public and what is private. And pollution, being a recent culturally perceived phenomenon, has been incorporated as belonging to the public's domain, not as an individual's business.

A second level of perceiving pollution has come about in recent years and that has to do with the expansion of knowledge, on the one hand, and communications, on the other. Knowledge means the establishment of a worldview based on scientific research and theories about the environment. In this sense environment is a concept that was created only recently. It differs from nature in many ways, the most obvious of which is that it can be dealt easily in terms of quantities. Now communications means the diluted transmission of this view through mass media. In this regard the Dutch have certainly had their fill of programmes, campaigns, reports, shows, analyses, graphs, theories, in short, all the paraphernalia that is allowed to go on such media. They know enough what acid rain means, where smog comes from, what nuclear energy does to a person. TV reports showing lascerating burnings of forests, massive oil spills on the ocean and thick black smoke clouds rising out from factory chimneys have a strong effect on people especially in helping them perceive the relation between their own environment and all the other environments in the world. The world has in this way become objectified as one, more so than at the time when there were colonies abroad and European dominance was self-evident.

But, as with commercial advertisements, the psychological and philosophical end results of environmental communications and campaigns are of short duration. Even when information comes as recriminatory lecturing that means to remind people that they are partially responsible for what is being described, it tends to catch their attention for a certain time span and then be processed as so much disposable material.

Seeing dead fish lying on the ocean shore or finding out that noble birds of prey are no longer nesting in Dutch territory is the type of thing that makes eveyone sorry and concerned. "Silent springs" had been happening for a long time in Holland and in Europe but it was not a determinant factor in awakening Dutch feelings of alarm over impending environmental disasters.

What really turned their attention on was nuclear power. It did so both in the form of threats of warfare – and even today every first Monday of the month at midday a siren is switched on all over the country to remind people of a possible nuclear attack – and in the form of accidental leakages from nuclear plants. The disturbing sights of Hiroshima and Nagasaki and the threat of cancer began to sediment down people's minds in such a way that when the Three Mile Island leak occurred in the United States and Chernobyl spewed up its noxious vapours into the atmosphere and contaminated grazing animals in Holland, nuclear energy disasters became very real to everyone and moved people into action.

Pressed by the antinuclear movement and by their constituencies, politicians, political parties, and government began to take a firmer stand on the issue. So much so that the programmes that had been set out to build nuclear power plants through the 80s on were halted if not practically cancelled from near future considerations. One strong motive that helped make this decision easy for government and industry were the gas fields that began to be exploited in the mid 60s and which proved to be big enough to meet some 55% of the country's energy needs for at least 50 years to come. The impact of the no nuclear plants decision was nevertheless very important for Holland to step out in the forefront of the environment movement and be recognized in many countries as environmentally wise, even though the issue has not been resolved in a definite manner as Holland – through Urenco company – continues to be an important industrial producer of nuclear fuel for its two nuclear power plants and for other such plants in other countries. On the other hand, people that had been working hard in antinuclear campaigns were demobilized and even NGOs that had sprouted up in the 70s and had thrived on account of their radical stances now had to expand their focus of interest in order to maintain themselves on par with the environment movement.

Concern and consequently action against nuclear energy moved Europeans and Dutch people in a way that dead fish had not – and only occasionally seals and the ubiquitous whales could. Nuclear power concerns have waned somewhat in recent years and particularly in Holland. So much so that it is not even included in the recent reports or agendas of either government or NGO's. Nevertheless it was nuclear fear that opened pandora's box of environment evils and consequently provoked environmental awareness. From then on a long and seemingly never-ending list of environmental problems began to surface and to impress people. These problems range across the whole spectrum of nature's elements – fire being the least conspicuous here (that seems to be *our* problem) – as well as man-made institutions, like their own homes, not to speak of the refuse of human and animals alike, with special reference to cows, pigs, and chickens.

For many people these problems are identified now as modern evils, the very beasts of Apocalypse. Although the final products of the historical development of Western civilization, and often seen as temporary problems that that civilization will eventually take care of, they nevertheless seem to threaten its very *raison d'être,* if not its survival and the survival of humanity itself.

These are impressions that we feel pervade the sensitivity of the majority of Dutch people to their environment and to this universal issue. Of course no one can say that there is a consensus view – even in a society that prides itself on its consensual way of disputing and settling questions – on the environment issue. Dutch society is after all sufficiently diversified, if not divided, along several lines – class, economic interests, religion, regional peculiarities, etc – to produce a consensus view of a question that is perceived in so many different ways and degrees.

But the points in common are many and are very neatly presented, at least as the far as diagnosis of the problem is concerned. Three or four major governmental policy reports lay out the issues, the statistics, the scenarios, the prognoses with full force and integrity. They are fairly well accepted as truthful by industry and agriculture groups and by the larger society – including most NGOs. But when it comes to presenting solutions to these problems the consensus cracks up and when it boils down to action implementation then havock and disarray take over.

The people

The light eyes and light hair that one observes in the great majority of Dutch people reflect a high degree of biological homogeneity in the country. Except for immigrants and the descendants of Spaniards, who have long been incorporated in the mainstream of the gene pool, there is not much human biodiversity around. Cultural homogeneity is also a fact although an anthropologist would soon find out that there are significant differences in culture between the South and the North, between city and country people, between Protestants and Catholics. Not enough to cause problems of cultural antagonisms that plague other countries, but significant to the point of representing man's capacity to be constantly creating and maintaining cultural peculiarities as marks of sociocultural identities. Nevertheless many concerned people feel that the cultural homogenizing process that has been intensifying in the last two or three decades of modernizing the country is definately wiping out the traditional cultural ways of many re-

Bicycles on the Dam in Amsterdam. (Photo Michel Pellanders/HH)

gions, towns, and even districts that once were so important in maintaining the cultural identity of the people.

Many Dutch intellectuals talk about "pillarization" as a social process that best categorizes Dutch social divisions. According to the pillarization theory Dutch society is organized and identified along vertical lines, each of which represents a social pillar, a population segment characterized by common interests and worldviews which would be unique in themselves and distinct from others. The most traditional pillars would be the Protestants, the Catholics, the industrial and business people, the agriculturalists, the labour organizations, and so on. Interestingly enough the Friesians, the only ethnic group that stands apart from Dutch mainstream, do not fit into the pillarization theory but are nonetheless recognized as distinct in many regards and with a unique potential in relation to the rest of the Dutch people. Although many in number, categories such as school teachers, state functionaries, etc, are not recognized as constituting social pillars in their own right.

Taken to its logical consequences pillarization theory should recognize as many social categories as there are distinct interest-oriented groups. These groups would relate to one another in either conflictive or complementary ways depending on the circumstances, but they would not necessarily or intrinsically be antagonistic to one another. In an historical sense this is a variation of the theory of corporativism and as such it is an attempt to both represent the dynamics of the formation of a nation as well as to meet the challenges posed by Marxist class theory. This report is obviously not the place to discuss this question up but it was deemed pertinent to bring it out, as an example that points out the important divergencies within Dutch society and Dutch sociopolitical views.

There is, on the other hand, no doubt that Dutch society is also structured as a class society. Or in other words, its socioeconomic system, despite its advanced stage in equalizing incomes and opportunities for all and in improving political democracy, has not as yet overcome the important contradictions between the main categories that define capitalist society as a system. The fact is that there are many ways and means in which the Dutch relate to one another and therefore create particular worldviews, or distinct variations of a common worldview, and have divergent opinions and positions on issues such as the environment.

Keeping this caveat in mind we can proceed to a descriptive analysis of a generalized Dutch view on environment.

Self-assurance or how things can be taken care of

In an enlightening interview we had with a well-known Leiden University social psychologist who has done extensive work on Dutch views on environment, we discussed these views in relation to what the Dutch would be willing to do to improve these bad conditions. Comparing these notes with other observations we had been making on Dutch feelings towards their own culture and the environment issue, we came up with a view of our own on this matter (which can not be of course our kind professor's responsability).

First of all, it is clear that the Dutch have a sense of pride in their political culture which means in their capacity for work and for finding negotiable solutions to their problems. They have a particular sense of practicality that denotes both self-assurance and a trust of others, including, of course, government. But, in contrast perhaps to Germans, the Dutch don't always feel that government policies and regulations are correct. That allows them some margin for manoeuvering which can range from the simple disregard of a seemingly absurd regulation or policy position to outright civil disobedience. This underlining psychocultural characteristic gives the Dutch a special feeling of rationality that is not encumbered by the rigourness of logics. This gives them a feeling of tolerance of one another's personal faults that is easily seen in the way they accept the use of light drugs and don't condemn so harshly hard drug users and in the way they condone minor misdemeanors, such as bike thefts. Practically every person has had a bike of his own stolen at least once and often he recovers it by catching the thief himself and taking it back with minor quarreling.

Those are positive expressions of Dutch nonchalance. In terms of the environment issue and the dangers it poses, this nonchalance shows up both as a trust that things will eventually be taken care of and as a disregard for the seemingly long term possibilities of disasters taking place. The nuclear energy threat apart, of course.

Take, for instance, the looming greenhouse effect threat. The Dutch have every reason to have a strong interest on this issue. After all, 60% of their country is situated under sea level. And the practical explanation of the warming up of an environment can easily be seen in their own greenhouses. Yet, according to our professor's enquiries, this threat is perceived as having a possible deleterious effect only in a fairly distant future. Thus it surprises any non-Dutch to realize that this people have no fear that their lowland country is protected from the sea by only a system of dikes and hydraulic canals. Their trust on their water control system is based on a 700 year long history, notwithstanding the 1953 Zeeland flood, but as far as we could gather God is not claimed as a voucher of the system.

However, disinterest in the greenhouse effect has less to do with self-assurance than with the sense that in order to do away with it or mitigate its results some important, almost drastic, changes would have to be considered and that would mean changing one's life style in a manner that would reduce some of the benefits that now represent important achievements to

60% of the country is situated under sea level. (Photo Evert Boeve)

individuals and the country alike. And that is very discouraging indeed. After all, these benefits have just been obtained in less than two generations' time and they have been increasing in an apparent exponential rate. How could anyone give them up particularly in view of the fact that no other people or nation intend to do so? This is an altogether understandable human attitude even from the point of view of those who do not enjoy these benefits or of those who have just begun to obtain them. Even people like Americans, who have been experiencing constant upgrading of their incomes and social benefits, would not easily give them up.

Home is where my car is

There are several groups of polluters which contribute to the greenhouse effect. Industry and agriculture play their part in it but the most visible contributor is undoubtedly the car. Would anyone dare throw the first rock at this? The Dutch and other Europeans have been willing to make some effort at improving gasoline consumption and the exhaust systems of their cars and will not feel extremely upset (as U.S. citizens would certainly) if some burden be placed on them to help achieve minimal emissions of CO_2 and other gases. The recent tax set by the government on oil prices, which is expected to reach US$ 10 a barrel by the year 2000 will probably be accepted with a sense of necessity, but will not scare consummers off their cars. The 25% increase in gasoline price will put minor pressure upon one's budget and will certainly be paid off by the normal income growth that is expected to take place in that same period of time.

Cars are the most fascinating objects of modern times. And behind them, the biggest and most flexible industrial complex works to make them more and more desired. They are both social and personal objects. They give people a sense of freedom and of control of their lives that no other tool can give. They are practical and at the disposition of their owners. They enhance the sexual appeal of the young and of the matured person. They are the best, the most visible symbols of one's position in life. For many people cars can even gain a sense of personality and they end up becoming pet-like creatures. And finally, according to consumer's behaviour polls, they are an extension of one's personality and one's home. After a tiresome day's work, people feel better when they get into their cars, turn their radios on to their favourite stations, smell their own car-like smells and drive home. It is cosier and apparently safer than the train.

How can they give up on this? When and by what means could Dutch people be willing to give up on having comfortable cars and on driving even when it is not necessary (less than 6 km a day to and from their jobs)? That is a question that few dare give an answer. For it seems that there has been enough campaigning on this for the Dutch to know best the betting stakes. And few believe that such instruments as "ecological education" are effective enough in the short run. And the question seems to be a short-run one. Or not?

Students of history find out that people have a particularly ungraspable way of dealing with their own problems and that although often they don't know the solutions, they find them by tact, by trial and error, by discussing them together with the whole range of their possible attitudes and worldviews. Maybe this is occurring now with the car issue. Some people are experimenting with different types of fuels, including electric and solar. Others use smaller, less oil-guzzling cars. Still others have long been trying to shift people's attentions to bicycles or even motorbikes. In short, as this is not a particular country's problem but rather a trait of a whole civilization everywhere, people are beginning to get the feeling that something has to be done about this golden calf or else they will be irretrievably caught by the spell of this Pied Piper like whistle that is enticing them towards oncoming disaster.

What do I do with my old bike?

The question of old bikes, broken TVs and worn out couches is a very serious matter. There are more of those on the streets of Amsterdam than there are abandoned children on the streets of Rio de Janeiro. The country just does not have enough space to afford making dump sites in one in every two cities like you find in the U.S. Moreover, most of the waste material is harmful to the environment and usually nondegradable. Cases in point are batteries, plastics, and foams, but there are the more manageable ones like paper, glass bottles and tin cans. The recycling of all these materials can eventually be achieved some time in the near future if only it proves viable for people to spend time taking these things to the proper places and if new industries reuse and turn them out more cheaply.

But what is to be done with upholstery that goes out of style or coats that one gets tired of and simply does not want to keep anymore. That is a problem that goes beyond technical solutions and has to do incisively with the question of consumerism, or the psychocultural drive to consume more and more of the goods that one's society presents. The problem seems to get even more difficult even when one realizes that this drive is the very fundament of that society and of its richness. To cut it out would amount to making that society unviable. So if until recently people were encouraged to work hard and consume lots, now that they have plenty of money to spend they are being told to be modest and stick to the essentials. Of course, only a small minority practices this kind of cultural rationing and position. The full consequences are not yet seen by the Dutch common person. But when the time comes will they take it seriously?

Tap water is good for drinking but not rainwater

Maybe Dutch people and Europeans are already used to it but the visitor is astonished to find out that the water that drops from the clouds is not suitable for drinking. Recycled water from sewage is also safe, even for the Queen if one overlooks the contained disgust face she made as she was offered a drink of it in a public ceremony.

Acid rainwater, with a Ph level of 4.5, does not actually precipitate as rain but as dry fall. So it does not help if you hurry from the rain to avoid your hair become acidic; it will get that way anyway. But you can always use tap water and a nice biodegradable shampoo to clean it. However, the acid water that precipitates on trees is not easily washed off but rather oozes into them in a way that ends up killing them, or, in a strange sense, making them suffer.

It is said that 40% or more of the tree cover of Holland is irreversibly damaged by acid rain. Some of those trees were pointed out to us and we were given a quick biological lesson

Self service. (Photo Theo Audenaerd/HH)

on the signs of the permanent disease of those sick trees. It was not too hard to recognize sick trees after a while but all the same it was easy enough to be distracted by the fact that most of them were still green looking, did not stink, or seemed smaller.

This is probably how an average concerned Dutch person behaves when seeing one of those rare wood patches or what could in some vague sense be called a natural area. If he likes to make comparisons he could think of countries that fell and burn trees to make farm land and conclude that acid rain is just as bad, but nevertheless not particularly bad. After all, Dutch sick trees still stand up and who knows if they shall not be cured someday.

Likewise acid water precipitation has for quite some time been damaging many of the old and revered monuments and sculptures that are so important for the cultural heritage of the country. Considerable efforts and money have been invested in repairing the damages and the results are very noticeable. So in the end people can renew their optimism that things will be taken care of.

Give me a Friesian and I will feed the world

Cows are not sacred in Holland as they are in India. They do not roam about but rather they are kept in confinement, groomed and overfed because they produce a lot of milk and quite a bit of meat. It is said that a Dutch cow costs over US$ 2,000 a year, a personal income that few Third World countries have per capita. Cows, pigs, and chickens, together with the production of potatoes, beets, and other vegetables make Holland the second biggest agricultural exporter in the world, and that is quite a feat for such a small country. Much of this is the result of traditional Dutch farming competence coupled with their traditional highly developed mercantile culture. Dutch farmers and the Dutch government know that capital investment is important to keep productivity up and that has allowed them a considerable competitive edge over other also important traditional farm cultures. Nowadays Dutch farmers can hardly be considered a particular sociocultural category, but are rather part of a more general category of small to medium scale industrial business people. And this category is becoming more and more dominated by medium scale enterprises as competition forces small farmers out of the market.

To maintain this competitiveness is an important stratetegic element in Dutch policy. It is not easy to touch on this issue when it relates discussing environmental degradation.

Many people in Holland are aware that the price of their food is among the cheapest in the world. Bananas are very cheap and they know that bananas are not grown in Holland but come from somewhere in the Third World. But potatoes are also cheap and they are grown here. They are cheap because, among other even more important but less known reasons, the soil is good and productive, ferlized and pest-controlled. The Dutch know that Dutch farmers use a lot of fertilizers and pesticides in their lands and that this overuse causes the presence of toxic substances in the vegetables which is not good for one's health. So what do they do about it? Nothing, or nearly nothing.

Organic farming is spreading slowly in Holland. Less than one percent of Dutch farms do not use non-organic fertilizers and pesticides. Their productivity amounts to less than 60% of that of a "normal" farm. Besides, for an unexpected strategic policy decision those farms do not receive any governmental funding or support, or even loans at normal farm interest rates. Consequently food produced on those farms costs twice or three times as much as from other farms. So people find it difficult to spend double their usual income percentage on such food, even though it is generally considered better for the health.

This is just about the range of understanding Dutch people have on the issue of farming in relation to environment. Few know the extent of the overuse of chemical fertilization and pesticides and that the top layer of farm soil like an Amazonian soil exposed to a rain storm is practically unuseable. The difference here is that it is not washed out but rather it should have to be scraped off and dumped somewhere. Furthermore, few people have a clear perception of what the high levels of concentration of toxic substances in the soil mean. They understand even less that the toxic substances have been leaching and will continue to leach into the groundwater for many years, making it practically undrinkable. But what after all be concerned about underground water if at the end it can be treated and you can drink it from the tap?

Environment abroad

Sixty percent or some 2.400.000 hectares of Dutch land are used for agricultural purposes. That is less than a third of what is needed for what they produce and export. That is mainly because much of what their farm animals eat, soya and tapioca, comes from other countries, principally Brazil and Thailand. So it seems Holland is using other people's land as a first step in their agribusiness. This, together with the cheap price fix on farm and mineral products, is the basis of modern colonialism. Few Dutch people use and fewer still agree on this argument. Certainly neither government nor businesspeople. This matter can be more clearly explained in terms of the market, on the one hand, and in less kind words about the character of those nations, on the other. Particularly their incapacity "to get their act together", as a government official once put it. So what could people possibly have to do with it?

The connection between Dutch economy and environment abroad is not understood by Dutch people in any political way. Why bananas are cheap, why there is famine in Africa or why the Amazon is burning are not questions that have anything to do with the well-being of Dutch society or even with Dutch pollution. The Dutch may have a certain feeling that it may affect them somehow, but not in any immediate sense. What is most usually understood is the argument that if it were not for the import of Third World agricultural commodities those countries would have a harder time surviving.

However, a link has recently been made between home environment and Third World environment in the argument that the Dutch environment is being affected by the introduction of too much animal fodder which is transformed into goods but also into waste. The Dutch are importing waste from Third World countries. This is actually a trial argument. Environmental NGOs are testing if it is effective in convincing Dutch people that they should be self-sufficient in food production even if that means decreasing their productivity.

This is the counterpart of an earlier argument, which asked Dutch consumers to boycott import foods that come from countries controlled by undemocratic governments, or that benefit only their high class, or else that the production of those foods causes environmental degradation, or that threaten the survival of minority groups. This whole set of political arguments and positions is presented in a way that causes confusion in people's minds. These are never clear issues and as a matter of fact they just beat around the bush without ever bringing out the rabbit. In the end people end up confirming their previous biases and preconceptions about Third World countries and their problems. Why are rainforests being burnt if not either because of the greed of backward if not degenerate farmers who cannot see further than a foot ahead of their noses, or because the mad policy of corrupt governments? At best it is because these countries have gotten themselves in so much debt that it is their only way keeping up with payments. And the foreign help is always squandered off by a leacherous group of corrupt politicians and their middle class counselors.

The Museum of the Tropics

One might think preconceptions exist as natural inherent traits that one culture transmits from generation to generation. Sometimes one can actually trace their origins back to some intercultural incidents that motivated their creations. Colonialism, especially the nineteenth century variety, is very rich in ordering European biases against their former colonies in particular and against what are now known as Third World countries in general.

However, if they are to survive, preconceptions need to be remembered and recalled and taught again and again. And in newer and better ways compatible with the thinking and the attitudes of the new generations. The Museum of the Tropics, we are sorry to say, is the institutional epitome of Dutch bias against Third World countries. Of course, it is not anything as outrightly grotesque as the Paris Museum de l'Homme, but it does have its way of putting up the wall between what one world is and what is the other and where truth and decency lie.

Although lodged in a nice and pleasant building the Museum of the Tropics contains, to begin with, so much stuff per square centimetre that it feels like a parody of Dutch density, not Third World vastness. As a matter of fact, one of its main information themes is the population explosion. Secondly, the written captions that are intended to explain the pictures and photos convey not only the feeling of exoticism, which is in some way understandable, but also of the irrationality and helplessness of the people depicted. The message is, the people could only be saved by the rightful hand and counsel of Europe. The section on African decolonization disgraces all African nations and gives the clear opinion that not only would they be better off had they been wise enough to maintain their colonial status, but that they never will be able to pull themselves out of the economic and political mire they have gotten themselves into. Why are native tribespeople somewhere in a Southeast Asian island losing their lands and their cultures to the power-saw weilding lumber companies which are devastating the forest, when the fact that some of those companies are Dutch investments and the lumber is also to come to Holland itself is never mentioned?

One cannot leave the Museum of the Tropics without feeling that the world in the tropics is sad, as a famous French anthropologist once put it, but also sore, and that it abodes ominous threats to humanity.

Shell Pernis. (Photo Jan Lankveld/HH)

Noxious German and other European gases and fluids

The Mexican saying about the United States – "so far away from God, so close to the United States" – could be applied to Holland in relation to Germany and was probably so applied at least once or twice in their history. In an environmental sense it certainly has to be used now as much on account of air pollution as of water. What is certain is that no matter how hard the Dutch could work to clean and maintain their environment the task will never be complete if the Germans do not decide to do the same. How conscious are the Germans about the environment? Are they cutting down on car use, industrial waste dumping in the rivers, particularly the Rhine, are they filtering their factory chimneys enough?

In other words, are the Germans willing to lower their

standard of living in order to meet Dutch regulations on environmental protection? These are not rhetorical questions but are constantly being brought to the fore of NGO discussions and international government disputes. Recently, as Holland performed the perfunctory role of chair of EC, it realized just how far Europe is from a common understanding on general regulations on environmental control. The agreement to accept a US$ 10 levy on a barrel of oil in order to create a fund for environmental protection in case of accidents is hardly a decisive step in view of the pressing regulations Dutch official reports call for.

Would the French be of any help, or the British, the Spaniards, the Italians, perhaps the Belgians? Some Dutch environmental activists feel that the great deal of exaggeration and boasting about their environmental consciousness and political decision is uncalled for. They feel that the government indeed has been very wise at PR manoeuvering but that given the state of the Dutch environment they are dangerously behind on developping a environmental control schedule and decision making.

But so, proportionately, is the rest of Europe, with the honourable exception perhaps, in the view of some Dutch, of the Scandinavian countries. These are actually the only countries and cultures that the Dutch look upon with ease and socio-environmental respect. But they also know that these countries cannot serve as models, if ever Dutch NGO people felt in need of one, because Scandinavians have the advantage of having a more balanced population density. So the Dutch have to appeal to their innermost resources, as ought any brave people.

The Greenies are coming

NGO people are both serious and warm-hearted, as are people of the 60s generation. In the Netherlands as elsewhere in the world they represent a social segment that is the outcome of what some sociologists call post-modern society. That type of society, or of social relations, can be found even in Third World countries, albeit in small proportions of their total populations. Some anthropologists and philosophers wonder if they do represent a sort of vanguard, to put it in an old-fashioned term, of the civilization that produced them, or the negation of that civilization as it moves on to transcend itself. Whatever the case, NGO activists are not middle of the road people, so their views are seen as different and not easy to be agreed upon by the common citizen. Besides, government policy and business interests are often in outright confrontation with those views. And when not they are always a step behind.

The NGO environmental movement has a publicly visible history of some twenty or so years. In this time it has achieved a few important victories and made some solid contributions to governmental policy and to the opening of people's mind about their lives. It is said that in the Netherlands some 1,5 to 2 million people contribute in some way to the environmental movement. The bulk of this contribution, however, boils down to demonstrating sympathy and handing out money to the more overt campaigns, particularly those in defense of endangered animal species or against nuclear power. That is how the environmental movement got started and become known. But the movement has really moved far ahead of its original goals and now demands a type of commitment that comparatively few people can engage in. It seems that the movement has now reached a sort of saturation point in which the investments do not get satisfactory or proportionate returns either in mobilizing and convincing people or in pushing the government toward political and administrative action.

As a consequence some NGO people have recently become more and more hard-minded in their political stands and styles of life. They know or seem to know how much they can expect from their own people, from business interests, and from the government. And they are not satisfied with that. They are pretty sure of the value and importance of their cause and are willing and have demonstrated how much sacrifice they can take to push it on. Some of them have acquired a certain air of quasi-religious commitment which somehow does not seem much in the tradition of Dutch culture. Except in so far as this attitude is restricted to personal decisions, as for instance, in becoming vegetarian or refusing to drive cars. Even then they are performed in modest and discrete ways.

On the other hand, there are very few communitarian experiments in the country, so collective radical stands are not there to be followed or emulated. That may be why the Dutch environmental movement is so keen in elaborating a critical discourse of the interrelations between environment, peace, and Third World questions but not in puting out a practical programme to, say, cut down on car use.

Examples such as the Max Havelaar "sustainable" trade and the De Kleine Aarde project are important as illustrations of collective action and they will be discussed in the next chapter. Other experiments in Dutch collective environmental action so far have not achieved the same level of consolidation. On Texel Island, for instance, a popular beach resort area where there is also an important centre for the study and rehabilitation of seals, a NGO has been trying to convince farmers not to use chemical fertilizers in their crops. Results of this work are still slim. Given the sources of the island's income, for a foreign visitor it could seem ideal to regulate if not prohibit altogether not only the use of fertilizers and pesticides but also of cars, were it not for the domineering short-sighted market oriented nature of Dutch political decision making process.

Chapter 3

Agriculture, transport, and industry

Introduction

The Netherlands is known all over the world as a country that has a high technology industry, intensive arable and livestock farming and one of the densest motorway networks with a very high car use per head of the population. These activities, apart from making the country rich and overdeveloped, also make it one of the most heavily polluted countries in Europe if not in the world. This was admitted by a former State Secretary for Environment a few years ago and has since intensified everyone's concern for environment in the country. The environmental crisis (global warming, acid rain, toxic waste, desertification and deforestation) is brought about by the Western process of development and is a threat to humankind. This is something that every Dutch person knows for the environmentalists have been on it for the last twenty years. The National Report to UNCED 1992 also shows that there is a relatively high level of awareness on the seriousness of the environmental problems facing the country. It is purported to be the number one concern of the Dutch citizen as of 1990. However, from this there does not follow equal commitment to take measures in control of these problems.

Why are the Dutch people resistant to change? Is it really because the decision-making process in the Netherlands is based on consensus or is it that the Dutch do not want to stand in the way of their economic progress, namely growth, technological innovation and accumulation of wealth?

As it appears that since the majority of the Dutch people are unwilling to change their style of life, the policy plan will have but a technological adjustment and patch up. Bill McKibben in his book *End of Nature*, argues that, "It is not enough just to state the horrifying implication of the damage to the ozone layer and to the dangers of the greenhouse effect. An action should be taken." He offers a choice: on the one hand we can ignore the implication of what we have done – that is, to refuse to accept the responsibility. We can abandon nature altogether, using science and technology to create a synthetic paradise which is genetically spliced into arid perfection. Or we can abandon our pride and insistence on man's supremacy over the planet and acknowledge our obligation. We cannot restore what we have already destroyed but we can limit the damage and in so doing try to ensure our future and that of the planet.

Environmental problems cannot be permanently solved technologically, because technological manoeuvring is in most cases an "end of the pipe solution" and therefore very expensive. It is a continuous measure, or as Milbrath puts it: "Technological fixes are applied to fixes that were applied to fixes."[1] So we can go on fixing what was fixed and in the end encounter disaster, e.g. nuclear accidents and fast depletion of natural resources such as fossil fuel, rainforests and minerals. There will then be a scramble for the short-term increase in output and the big powers, as usual, will use all the means (money/military) to grab the lion's share, forcing the poor nations to die a natural death from poverty and hunger. Where is the equity? Is there any alternative to this?

This chapter will deal mainly with the limits and timetables set by the Dutch government on agriculture, transport and industry. At the end, a few possible alternative views will be presented in the form of proposals toward contributing to the possible solutions to some of the environmental problems described.

Agriculture

1. A few facts

According to the Netherlands National Report to the UNCED 1992 the agricultural sector has achieved a dramatic increase in productivity. Its contribution to the national income is estimated at 12.5% (1988) with the employment of 475,000 labour years. Many of the products are exported through the European Community market, strengthening the country's balance of trade. Through this increase in production the Netherlands has managed to snatch a high place as the second largest exporter of agricultural produce in the world. On one hand the government has played a greater part in increasing production. It has encouraged the ratio of larger agricultural enterprises through scale expansion for economical reasons as well as prestige. This has led to specialization and intensification of farm practices which has resulted in monoculture farming, especially in corn for animals and in tulips. Under such practices the crop becomes vulnerable to pests and disease. Thus the use of high doses of fertilizers and pesticides become inevitable. The Netherlands holds the world record for agricultural pollution, an average of twenty kg of pesticides per hectare per year. Germany only uses four kg per hectare per year.[2]

There has been a reduction in the number of farmers from 162,000 in 1975 to 108,000 in 1986. This is mainly due to the inability of small farmers to compete. A further 50% reduction is expected by the year 2000 if this type of high technological farming is continued.

The growth in production is also the result of guaranteed purchases by the EC of large numbers of products at a fixed price. Consequently there have been structural surpluses and a system of subsidies which take up 65-75% of the EC budget. However, the pressure on land has been causing severe damage to the environment and that has been estimated to cost 6.1 billion Dutch guilders per year. Consequently this has forced a decline in agricultural financial balance of -4.5 billion guilders per year. This means that had the environmental costs been reflected in agricultural production, the Dutch people would have been paying more for their food items.

The Netherlands is also a great importer of raw materials for its agro-industry. 15-16 million hectares of land in other countries is under production for Dutch needs, including animal feed. The South provides about 5 million hectares of land for this purpose. For each Dutch cattle farmer there are a number of farmers in the South tilling for him. This surely can be considered a type of modern servitude, if not slavery. The prices for these crops are often too low to guarantee a sustainable development in the Southern countries. More land each year in the South is taken from food crops to cash or export crops leaving the poor people with less to eat. Most of the imported animal feed is lost through the digestive system of the animals. Only 20% of the vegetable protein fed to animals is converted to animal protein.[3]

Excess manure. (Photo Martijn de Jonge/HH)

High production of manure is one of the major crises in the agriculture sector in the Netherlands. About 110 million tons of manure from 120 million farm animals are produced yearly; out of which only one half is used in agriculture. So much of it is lost to the environment, where it pollutes the soil, drinking water and the air and causes acid rain.

Energy consumption in the production of agricultural products is very high. About 143 petajoules (peta = one million billion) a year is used and 80% of it is used in heated glasshouses to produce summer crops in winter.

2. Agricultural policy

The agricultural policy laid out in the Netherlands' National Environment Policy Plan 1990-1991 is based on the idea that agriculture is an economic activity carried out by individual enterprises and that it produces goods which are safe for consumption without causing irreversible damage to the physical environment which is its natural resource. In other words, here is that, the priority is food production and environment is of secondary importance. However, as part of the effort to create a sustainable agriculture system, the policy has set targets for the use of surplus manure and fertilizer, which are considered the major problems in agriculture. These targets can be summarized as:

a. to reduce the discharge of phosphates and nitrates from manure to the North Sea by 25% by the year 2000.

b. to reduce ammonia emission by 70% by partly taking the surplus manure to the areas of shortages and partly processing the manure to get dry fertilizer. 20 million tonnes should be processed yearly by the year 2000.

c. the quantity of manure produced should be reduced by changing the composition of the animal feed and altering feeding methods.

d. to reduce the level of phosphate in animal manure to a maximum of 7.4 kg per animal per year. The production use of phosphate and nitrogen-poor fodder is being stimulated by expanding the application of the minerals inputs registration in conjunction with the agricultural industry.

e. by the year 2000 maximum use should be made of crop protectors which are not harmful to man and the environment. The use of pesticides, expressed in terms of kilograms of active ingredients per year, will be reduced by 50% and no substances will be admitted which are regarded as detrimental to the environment.

f. the use of pesticides can be reduced by using more stringent crop rotation and by developing and using organic crop protectors, e.g. parasites or predators.

All these proposals put limits that are far below the ecologically required reduction of emissions which are: ammonia 90%; pesticides 90%; NO_x 80%.

3. Limits to such remedies

The problem of surplus manure and high usage of toxic chemicals in the name of fertilizers and pesticides is very great and very real. Though the government has set out targets for reducing the pollution caused by this sector, it remains doubtful whether the objective will be achieved within the given period, and this is also the feeling of many environmental groups in the Netherlands. The manure surplus problem is brought about by massive cheap imports of livestock feeds partly from the Third World to meet the demand of the ever growing intensive livestock farming. So, as long as the number of cattle increases there is no way the policy plan can be effective. In the first place the idea of transporting the manure to arable land in Europe does not meet the objective of closing the mineral cycle. Thus the farmers of the Third World who depend on livestock feed for export will go on degrading their land through forest clearing and monocultures for export crops. In this case, more resources flow to the rich, widening the gap between the rich and the poor even further.

Secondly, the intensification of the farming system will lead to an increase in the number of animals as long as the amount of phosphate in the manure per animal remains the same.

Consequently in the end the total amount of phosphates will still be high. Manure storage and processing could be a solution but only temporarily. The energy use will be high and the bulk too big to transport to far-off places. Animal keeping will become too expensive and more farmers will be forced out of business.

The farmers we interviewed showed a great deal of concern for the manure issue – especially the quota system. It makes them unable to move their animals from one farm to another. They feel that the government people demand too much of them, which makes them hesitant to invest more, in fear of more regulations. They showed a feeling of resentment. Once they were the celebrated few who fed the population cheaply, but now that there is a problem, everybody is pointing a finger at them, and more so than at car owners or big industries.

These farmers are willing to change their system of production to more environmentally sound practices like free-range poultry and mixed farming – but this is not economically possible for them. The prices for the food crops in the Netherlands are very low and the only way to make ends meet is through intensive production. They are paid for quantity rather than quality. That is how the market works. Moreover, the position of the Netherlands in the European Community prevents the Dutch from choosing environmentally friendly agriculture.

The levels of toxic material used in agriculture is increasing due to the production of the special varieties as requested by industries. Crops like potatoes, both industrial varieties and food varieties like the Bintje, have brought a lot of problems to the farmers, to an extent that many of them are switching to the poultry industry. To grow potatoes successfully, 50 kg per hectare of pesticides are needed compared to other crops which would need only 4-5 kg per hectare. Such crops, though high yielding, are very expensive to produce and highly detrimental to the soil and drinking water. The use of another variety and crop rotation practices would have been the best solution to

Dutch polders, which are reclaimed land, can also be used for nature reservations. (Photo Evert Boeve)

this. However the farmers are somehow put in a position where they fail to make a choice due to dependence on agroindustry.

Farmers should be encouraged to go to De Kleine Aarde and learn the environmentally friendly farming practices. This institute carries out demonstrations on the best ways of farming and has high potential for changing the life styles of Dutch people if properly utilized. This can be taken as a step toward organic farming. Another possibility towards solving this could be to show the Dutch people, especially those in the farmers union, what is happening in the Third World; it might be a helpful sort of exchange programme.

4. Agriculture and nature

Agriculture in the Netherlands is simply another industry. Everything from land preparation to packing to the final product is mechanized. The smallest farmer in the Netherlands can be compared to the few large and prosperous farmers in Africa. Everything in these small farms is automized so as to reduce labour requirements. For example, one farmer in Wageningen needs only fourteen hours a week to attend five hundred pigs on his farm, so one can figure out how much fossil energy is needed to provide electricity for running these farms, not to mention the big farms. On average, the fossil energy used for heating, processing and transportation amounts to 143 PJ per year. 80% of this energy is used in glasshouses during the winter to produce summer crops. A decrease in glasshouse farming will help to reduce the energy consumption. This will also promote horticulture in the South.

Farming and nature have always been in conflict as far as land usage is concerned. About 70% of the land is in the control of farmers and the poor wild animals, especially the birds, have little place to establish themselves without threat to their lives.

The island of Texel is an interesting case in point. It is a resting ground for migrating birds during autumn. These birds, especially geese, eat a lot of grass in the paddocks which is grown for animals. The farmers are not happy so they shoot the birds and chase them away. The birds have to fly from one field to another and sometimes they are forced to fly far South. In doing so they use a lot of energy. Consequently, many die of fatigue and weakness. The survivors tend to eat more wherever they go in order to replenish what they have lost. Research has shown that farmers have been responsible for a big decrease in number of the birds which depend on peaty grasslands for food and nesting.

During spring these birds go nesting on the farms, but the farmers drain the land very early – making it difficult for the birds to get the worms to feed their young. Land preparation for early crops destroy a lot of nests, killing hundreds of young birds which are not able to fly. For some years now there has been a conflict between the farmers and the environmentalists on this issue. Farmers are interested in getting more than one crop for their farm animals so they are not ready to lose any to the birds. On the other hand, the environmentalists want to conserve nature because the birds and other animals have the right to live and have an important ecological function in eating millions of insects. Environmentalists are even ready to buy part of the land or compensate the farmers in a way for nature conservation but most of the farmers are not at all interested.

5. Alternatives observed in the Netherlands

Much effort has been made by NGO's here in collaboration with farmers and scientists in searching for suitable agricultural methods which are environmentally sound. Most of the work done presents good prospects because the problem has been well diagnosed and measures for controlling the situation have been put forward. It remains for Dutch people to decide whether to go on with the present way of production which has generally been recognized as very unhealthy, or to accept changes within their methods of production which will contribute to continuity, peace and security of the world. Dutch people should understand that the wealth they are enjoying is much greater than what the majority of the world can enjoy. They are able to do so because they are using more than their share of world resources and they can continue to be so if most of the world remains poor.

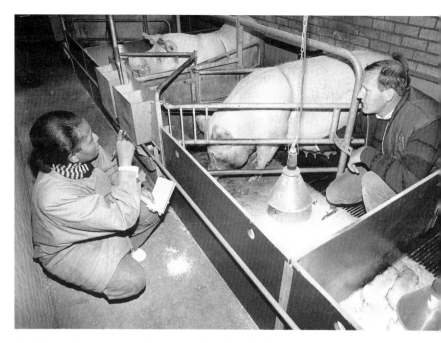

Sami Songanbele during an interview with a Dutch pig-farmer.
(Photo Ruud Gort)

Let us imagine a scenario in which the Dutch people continue their way in "business as usual". What could happen?

In "business as usual" the agricultural production in the Netherlands would lead to huge surpluses of cereals, potatoes and animal products. Consequently the prices would drop, especially those of cereals and potatoes which are already at the bottom. Arable farmers would then have to switch to horticulture where the methods of production are very demanding on toxic chemical use and energy consumption. Some farmers might decide to join intensive livestock farming, hence expanding the industry further, and calling for more imports of raw material for feed. The number of livestock per hectare would increase, therefore the surplus manure production would need surplus energy to control it. On the other hand, surplus production has a great impact on the limited world resources. More land in the Third World would have to be put under cash crops and less for food production, resulting in hunger and poverty. As more forest land is opened, more land would become vulnerable to erosion and the natural capacity of the world in CO_2 absorption by trees would be reduced.

In relation to peace, research has shown that fossil fuels will be depleted within a few generations, so the struggle between the developed nations for the supply of fuel would threaten global security. The Gulf War for example is nothing but a resource struggle. The US had made it clear long ago that they would go to war to secure their oil supplies and they have done it, without considering the effect of their weapons on innocent lives and on the environment. The increase in the levels of international tension would bring up once again the possibility of nuclear war. In the long run maybe the starving majority would follow their resources to the North most probably in big social conflicts.

In view of this imagined scenario it is unwise to create policies to reduce surplus production. This could be done through stabilization of production levels by using integrated methods of production where reduction in pesticide use can be achieved by changing the agriculture practices into organic farming or biodynamic farming. Here insects can be used as natural enemies to keep crop pests through predation or parasitism. A good example is the control of the cassava mealy bug in Africa by wasps. Also through organic farming, the number of livestock per unit area could be reduced and home grown cereals could be used to feed them. The manure produced would be used in the production of cereals.

Recent research on biodynamic (BD) agriculture by Berenschot[4] shows that the Netherlands can feed itself using BD agriculture and still will have surplus for export. Through this BD agriculture, emissions would be reduced by 76% of NH_3 (ammonia), 85% of NO_3 and 99% of PhO5 (phosphorus) and no biocides would be used. Of course there will be a slight reduction in production both in value and volume but then the environmental damage costs would be disposed of.

Perhaps the government could give the farmers moral and financial support via subsidies. Many farmers, especially young ones, show an interest in organic farming but see that their products become too expensive. Unless the "polluter pays" principle[5] is implemented only a limited number of people will buy their products. Farmers in Wageningen showed this fear of losing their income if they change to free-range poultry keeping. At the moment there are about 500 organic farmers in the Netherlands. Jan Juffermans of De Kleine Aarde is optimistic that this number will grow since many farmers foresee the problems of impact on environment if they continue with their conventional method of farming.

Another possibility which is also suggested by NGOs is the reduction of the number of livestock per unit area through preventing the new farmers from entering livestock farming. So the land which becomes available after the older farmers fails to get a successor can be put under afforestation or nature reserve. A legislative measure aimed at reduction of imported feedstuffs could also contribute substantially to reduce the number of livestock and amount of waste to acceptable limits. This will also help Third World people to have more land for their food production.

Dutch people should abandon their affluence and live simply so that others may simply live. There is no way that in the next century the majority of the world's population – 9.5 billion out of 11 billion – live in extreme poverty and only 1.5 billion people in the North live in abundance without political, security and moral problems arising. So if the Dutch people do not produce in a sustainable way, it will be like a snake biting its own tail.

Other additional policies promoted by NGOs also need government support. Things like market related policies, taxes on livestock, foodstuffs, imported and toxic chemicals, and motivation for organic farming are worth looking into. Subsidies granted for fossil energy (for glasshouses) and mechanization should be stopped, to reflect the real cost of conversion farming.

6. Conclusion

In view of the above discussion it is clear that with the same conventional method of agriculture there is no way the limit set by the government on emissions from agriculture will meet ecological sustainability. The only way is to cut off or reduce surplus production through the suggested means. The environmentalists in this country have done a commendable work in educating the public and rousing awareness on the issue of environmental damage. Through their pressure the government is now seeing the need for integrating the environmental policy into the agricultural sector. However, most of the things environmentalists say have met defensive reactions, because they challenge the cherished beliefs of the strong pillars, namely agribusiness and the multinational companies which have great influence in the country. They have managed to convince the population that through high technology everything is possible.

Industry

Since the late half of the 20th century industrial development in the Netherlands has taken new unprecedented forms. About 12% of Dutch land is occupied by industries. This development has raised the per capita income of the population, brought nobility and mechanization in many sectors. This prosperous life has brought about land destruction and pollution.

The industry sector in this country is highly energy intensive and is responsible for 50% of the total CO_2 emissions. Packaging material creates an enormous quantity of wastes and its incineration contributes greatly to the greenhouse effect and health hazards. Many farmers recently have been forced to pour milk in the drain for a long time due to dioxin contamination. These are toxic substances which are released on incineration of packaging materials. A lot of industrial wastes are dumped into rivers or on the ground causing a lot of poisoning in soil and water, disrupting the ecosystem and damaging health.

The presence of PCBs in the sea water, especially in the Wadden Sea, which constitute important spawning grounds for North Sea fish, has reduced reproduction in fish and consequently in seals as fish are their principal food. PCBs even in minute quantities such as one thousand of one millionth gram per liter of water are highly toxic and they are found in the breast milk of fish eaters like seals. Agricultural land is also heavily affected by pollutants which have been removed from surface waters such as heavy metals and non-biodegradable organics. In some areas owners of small plots of land are not allowed to eat vegetables from their land, due to the presence of heavy metals in the soil. So to them the only way of growing vegetable is the closed loop system in which soil is released of the burden but more energy is required.

One of the main world problems with chemical industries in the Netherlands is the major role they play in the production and consequently release of aerosol in the air, damaging the ozone layer. There is such an urgency in doing away altogether with the use of CFCs that the covenant under which CFCs production was planned to be banned by 1999 will have to go in effect much earlier.

Industry in the National Environment Policy Plan (1990)

The general objective for the target group industry is to develop an economically profitable industry which produces environmentally friendly products. Industry branches are given the following ceiling emissions as the guide line for the period of 1994-2000 for acidifying and eutrophication substances and they are allowed to formulate their own implementation plan. However they are expected to meet the following targets:

a. reduction of SO_2 by 80% by the year 2000
b. nitrogen reduction by 45%
c. VOCS (volatile organic compounds) should be reduced by 45-60%
d. phosphorus emission into surface water must be reduced by 50%
e. waste products must be also decreased substantially
f. CFC production must stop by 1999.

Limits to the Policy Plan

In accordance to the Netherlands non-government organization (NGO) report to the UNCED, this policy is a total failure. First, the target or emission ceilings set do not meet the necessary requirements. Secondly, the environmental plan attempts to reach the solution by dealing with results of pollution instead of the source of pollution (management strategy). The NGOs are not happy with this and they have a feeling that if consideration is not put on the choice of raw materials, on method and volume of production as well as on the nature of products produced then fundamental ecological restructuring of the sector will not be possible.

With management strategy, measures are taken too late when damage has already occurred, as in the case of the effects of CFCs on ozone layer depletion. Also recycling processes in most cases are extremely complicated and very expensive.

Another problem with this type of policy is the way industrial interest groups manipulate the situation. The "greening" of industry in the North – the use of high technology to improve the environmental impact of products – is done to maintain a firm's market share. This "environmental modernism" is carried out in the first place for economic and not ecological purposes. The multinationals are firstly interested in maintaining their status quo and new inventions are produced to either achieve this goal or when it is demanded by new regulations.

Dutch Transnational Companies in the Third World

The activities of the transnational companies are less controlled and regulated and have better lobbying power than the other sectors. This way they manage to manoeuvre their activities and avoid their responsibility of environmentally sagacious conduct. In many developing countries they have disrupted cultural and social economic life of the local people, depleted their land and left them starving.

Dutch transnationals: Third World Guide 91/92, p.437

Royal Dutch/Shell, a petroleum company of joint Dutch-British capital, is the largest non-American firm in the world. With a total 135,000 workers world-wide, the company had sales of US$ 85,52 billion in 1989. Besides extracting, transporting, refining and selling petroleum, Royal Dutch/Shell produces fertilizers and petrochemichals, and has interests, branches, and representatives in almost all capitalist countries.

Unilever, the world's largest maker of food and soap products. Of Dutch-British capital, it has headquarters in Rotterdam, London and New York. Unilever employs 300,000 workers around the world and had sales of US$ 35,28 billion in 1989. The company has Third World brances in the Dutch Antilles, Brazil, Chile, Colombia, El Salvador, Indonesia, Thailand, Tunisia, Venezuela and Zaire. Unilever licences its brand names and patents to local firms in almost all of the rest of the countries in Asia, Africa and Latin America.

Phillips Gloelampenfabrieken, electronics and household appliances. The company has 304,800 workers and had sales of US$ 26,99 billion in 1989. Third World subsidiaries in Brazil, Burundi, South Korea, Haiti, Hong Kong, India, Indonesia, Puerto Rico, Sout Africa, Uruguay, Zaire, the Phillipines, Malta, Mexico, Nigeria, Pakistan and Zimbabwe.

Akzo, chemical industries, with 70,900 workers and sales of US$ 8,84 billion in 1989. The company has numerous subsidiaries in Third World countries.

Other Dutch corporations listed in 1990 among the global 500 biggest are DSM, Hoogovens Groep, Heineken and Daf Trucks.

Possible alternatives

For sustainable industrial development, problems should be controlled from the source so that disaster does not take people by surprise. As a necessary first step industry should reduce the fossil fuel consumption in order to achieve CO_2 emission ceilings. Usage of raw materials should be given high consideration so that they do not interfere with land development in other countries and their final products do not turn out to be health hazards.

In order to have effective ecological restructuring, the NGOs propose that the government should exercise strict measures to make the industry comply to a time-scale in meeting the objectives of the policy plan. Given the power of industry lobbies the idea of group target consultations comes out as just one more way to give them a chance to continue their delaying tactics.

Individual and public transportation

The Dutch population density being so extremely high the burden on the natural environment of the concentration of traffic is enormous. Since 1986 mobility of Dutch population has increased greatly as a consquence of suburbanization and great prosperity. Car traffic has grown by 17% and the 15 million Dutch possess close to six million individual automobiles. This number is expected to increase to eight million by the year 2010 with a 35% increase of fuel consumption (RIVM).

The growth of traffic facilities account for an increasing demand on space and disintegration of landscape. After agriculture, traffic is considered the biggest contributor to the acidification problem as well as to the greenhouse effect. The main pollutants emitted by transport activities are hydrocarbons, lead, SO_2, NO_x, particulates. These have various adverse health and ecological effects. In addition transport is responsible for a number of deaths each year. Disposal of old cars (500,000/year) is another headache.

The Dutch railway system is already one of the most sophisticated and efficient in the world. The train services run twenty hours per day and may be seen as the major ally in the battle against congestion and environmental destruction. A growth of 35-100% is anticipated in 15 years to come.

Aviation is also one of the most efficient industries and means of transportation in Europe. A plan has been drawn to expand Schiphol airport into a European mainport. By 2003 the passenger traffic will double and air freight will increase considerably. However, besides high energy consumption air traffic also contributes to environmental damaging of the atmosphere and principally to the well being of the populations that live near airports.

Cars ready for the mulching machine. (Photo Martijn de Jonge/HH)

Policy Plan

The Netherlands urban and rural planning policy (VROM, 1988) adheres to the principle that the country must retain its important present economical position in Europe. This actually means that, in order to maintain this status quo, all changes should be directed towards industrial expansion to make the country more attractive to multinational companies. So what is expected is nothing but technical adjustments to the environmental pleas.

In relation to transportation the objectives of the National Environmental Plan (Plus), NEPP, are:

a. all vehicles through tax incentives and technological innovations must be as clean, quiet, economical, and safe as possible.

b. they should be made of parts and materials which are optimally suitable for re-use.

c. new ways for limiting the automobility so as to lower energy consumption and least possible pollution should be procured such as minimizing the need to travel between the place of work, shop, etc, and peoples' homes.

d. reduction in use of cars by private individuals and instead incentives on the use of public transport and bicycles.

e. funding public education and participation.

Emission ceilings

The NEPP has also set the following emission ceilings and targets for traffic and transport

- Equip passenger cars with three catalytic converters
- Use no more harmful substances in vehicles
- The raw material used must be able to be recycled for at least 85% in the waste stage
- Take structural measures to reduce the need for mobility
- Bicycles should be used for 5 km distances and trains for 200 KM

- Expand and improve bicycle routes and public transportation

	1986	2000	2010
NO_x passenger traffic[1]	163	40(-75%)	40(-75%)
NO_x goods traffic	122	72(-35%)	25(-75%)
Hydrocarbons passenger traffic	136	35(-75%)	35(-75%)
Hydrocarbons goods traffic	46	30(-35%)	12(-75%)
Carbondioxide	24.000	24.000(-0%)	21.600(-10%)
Noise passenger cars[2]	80	74	70
Noise lorries and buses	81-88	75-80	70
Number of houses[3]	260.000	130.000	4.000
Noise nuisance of any extent[4]	2.000.000	1.800.000	1.000.000(-50%)

Source (NEPP)

1. NO_x/C_xH_y in relation to 1980 (=100)
2. Target values for the maximum noise production of vehicles in dB(A)
3. Number of houses exposed to an unacceptably high noise level,
   reduced by 50% in 2000 through measures at source and in the transmission
4. Houses subject to noises loading of more than 55dB(A)

Limits to emission ceilings

The emission ceilings put in the NEPP shows that they are still below the necessary requirements, especially CO_2. Much in NEPP has been put under the mercy of high technology which has helped keep the Dutch cars clean, with low emissions and a considerable improvement in quality of the air. In this case then more technology above the present level is needed to pull the cealing emissions to the ecologically required levels. The expected growth of car volume to eight million by 2010 need to be considered. Despite the fact that all cars will be very efficient in fuel use as well as being fitted with catalytic converters for reducing emissions of lethal metals, still the enormous traffic volume and density threaten to overwhelm the improvements (Renner 1988).

Pollution control through technology is not as easy as it seems at first sight as research demonstrates. The so called efficient methods in reduction of CO_2 emission does in turn increase emission of methane which is a potent greenhouse gas. Also in controlling the CO_2 emission more energy is expended than would have actually been needed in driving the car. It is clear that by solving one problem we create another and then a new technology is required for to fix the first one.

According to Renner, technical solutions can generate a lot of excitement and attention because simple human adjustments can double the fuel-use efficiency and minimize the oil crisis. This however only occurs if the efficient car is used efficiently. In most cases, particularly in the Netherlands, the car carries only the driver or at most two people. Mostly cars are used here for shopping, going to work, or for leisure. In a year a Dutch car owner covers about 20,000 km at an average speed of 30 km/hour. This means that in a year he spends the equivalent to 74 days in his car, making it actually an extension of his home.

Behind the cars there are the biggest and most flexible industrial companies Western civilization has created. They are managed by the North. They put great effort into convincing people that cars are desirable and enhance people's personalities. Given the actual results it is difficult to imagine that car use can be cut down substantially by a sort of counter propaganda.

Traffic accidents are now among the leading causes of death in many of the developed countries. In the United States about 49,000 people die each year on the road. In the Netherlands about 1,500 people get killed through car accidents per year; although that may seem to be a low figure it contributes to the world toll in human life which was about 200,000 in 1985.

Car technology, though very promising, cannot in anyway ease traffic jams or serve the majority of people who will never own an automobile. Congestion is in most cases very annoying and uneconomical. More fuel is used while driving in cities at low speed due to rush hour paralysis of the traffic system. So far no country has come up with a solution to traffic jams because whenever they increase the roads more cars are attracted increasing pressure for more roads. According to the Memorandum on Traffic and Environment (1987) elaborated by the Ministry of Transport and Public Works, a reduction in NO_x emission by 50% can only be feasible if the volume of traffic, both private and commercial, is stabilized at slightly below today's levels.

The only efficient method so far in decreasing car use have been the oil crises. The economic and political vulnerability of a car dependent society becomes painfully clear when there is an oil crisis. In August 1990 when Iraq invaded Kuwait the whole North cringed and went crazy and the possibility of a third world war was raised once again. The damage caused by the Gulf War in terms of human lives, environmental pollution and the depletion of oil resource put the world in an awkward situation.

But the problem of cars in the Netherlands goes beyond environmental damage. Increased mobility requires more land for both parking and road construction. It is estimated that about one third of city land is devoted to roads, parking lots, and other infrastructures. This substantially reduces the area for those who do not have or cannot afford a car of their own.

A few obvious suggestions

In view of the above discussion it is clear that cars are a real problem in the Netherlands and that the Dutch driver will not easily give up on this modern marvel. So the only way to reduce car use is through hard provisions: to make unattractive conditions for driving such as less expansion of road facilities thus increasing congestion at rush hours. Also parking areas should be kept at a minimum and parking fees should be raised.

In order to enhance this measure public transport should be extra efficient. Buses, trains, trams, and metro are appropriate in many cities for fuel economy. Finally many small but viable incentives and facilities should be created to encourage the increase of bicycling, car pooling, and simply walking to and from one's job. Urban planning should be done in such a way as to enable the residential areas to be near the working places.

Notes

1   Milbrath,L. *Learning our way out.*
2   Source: Jan Juffermans, De Kleine Aarde
3   De Kleine Aarde
4   *Towards a Sustainable Agriculture?* Berenschot, 1990
5   The incorporation of the price of the environmental damage caused by a product into the price of that product – making the polluter pay.

Chapter 4

Hard problems, soft solutions

Holland: a calculated scene

The train starts out with a light jolt. As it moves along it introduces to us much of the country, giving clues to the ways the Dutch people live. It is a smooth train ride, the sway almost missing; so different from the wild shakebox we know in our own countries. Unfolding outside is a picture of order. Dainty cottages amongst small woods, neat farm homesteads, the greenest pastures imaginable dotted with plump and clean cows, alternating with straight lined patterns of paddocks filled with the brightness of flowers and uniform vegetable plots. Canals of water in abundance through each field.

Countryside gracefully blends into town and city. Here there are many factories, all look clean and in order. Cars and trucks glide by, leaving no trail – so many cars, yet not one of them is leaving a trail of black choking smoke behind.

Out of the station into the city of Amsterdam. Everything imaginable from different parts of the world is advertised enticingly in the glittering shops beckoning us to enter. We come to a flower shop and a psychedelic array of colour hits our eyes sending our senses reeling. Did we inhale too much of hashish fumes as we walked past a street of coffee shops? Has our perception been distorted? Every type of flower is there, shape and colour of each type uniform to the extent of exaggerated precision. The roses are to the red and the ferns just to the green. All very neat and calculated. Surely this could only be a dream.

Yet, it is reality, human made reality with all it takes. There is love here, there is hate, there is richness and misery. This country is made of earth, air, water, and humans, but we see little of mother earth. She is sealed from embracing us by hard pavements, asphalt and concrete. Here and there we encounter a calculated space of green or the bright colour of autumn leaves. Sometimes a glimpse of luxurious nature as the result of artful landscaping.

All this leaves many impressions on the beholder from the other world of less affluence. But the most impressive is the narrow view of nature. This in turn gives a totally different approach of seeing the problems the world faces today and a different set of proposals of solutions.

In search of a holistic view of nature

In the Southern indigenous holistic view nature is much more than the planet earth. It is the entire universe: the sun, moon, stars, atmosphere, ozone layer and all. From this perspective, nature will always create its own internal balance and harmony.

The human being is seen as but part of nature. It interacts within nature and should adapt to nature by controlling its own behaviour. Humans should not venture to disrupt natures constellation of harmony, because this would at the same time endanger themselves. Modernization as seen today is one example of how human activity can disrupt the harmonious balance of nature. This, however, does not mean that nature will remain unharmonious, it will always create its internal balance, but it could be that humans are wiped out of the scene, like so many other species, as a result of human activity.

The reluctance of humans to recognize nature as a holistic entity in which they themselves are only a small part results in misbehaviour which in turn results in what today are called "environmental problems". Thus environment is contrasted to nature in that the first is seen as cut up pieces that have only a rational thread to join them whereas nature is here seen in a holistic humanistic sense.

Nature from a Dutch perspective

What is seen as nature from a holistic point of view, in the modern view (Dutch) is a conglomerate of statistical numbers and use values:

a. The ozone layer in the stratosphere is of use because it absorbs part of ultraviolet radiation from the sun. Thus preventing humans from getting skin cancer.

b. Water is an essential factor of production in agriculture. Problems rise when consumption greatly exceeds supply.

c. Genetic diversity is of direct relevance to the maintenance of the productivity of agriculture crops and of options for the future. Nature includes between 5 and 30 million species, of which only 1.4 million have so far been described, and only a small fraction of these have been examined for their potential benefit to man.

All these examples are quoted from the document *A World of Difference*. There are many more examples along this line.

When parts of nature considered useful by humans are becoming of no use any more:

a. Soil fertility degrades, or on the contrary it becomes over fertilized.

b. Water is polluted, or the water table is sinking.

c. The loss of biodiversity is a problem because the agriculture will not have any genetic material to depend upon.

d. The ozone layer acquires holes and does not protect humans and useful parts of nature from the ultraviolet rays.

The conclusion, from a Dutch perspective, is that we have environmental problems. From a holistic point of view these are mere symptoms of a diseased nature. This fundamental difference in viewing nature results in a profound misunderstanding. While the holistic perception of "Nature Conservation" would ultimately mean adapting human behaviour from within – from the modern point of view it is: conserving little parts of territory that will remain untouched by the conquest of human activity on this planet earth.

"If the government presses the farmers, the farmers cut down the trees"
(Photo Evert Boeve)

From the holistic view it is a matter of the whole universe, from the modern view it could by any means be a patch of woods outside the city of Amsterdam, or a bit better, the Wadden Sea.

The whole reasoning behind why nature should be conserved is different. From the holistic view, nature conservation means "sustainability". From the Dutch view nature is among other things to be conserved in order to prevent the Dutch scenery from becoming monotonous. While nature to the majority of the Southern population is a matter of decent and dignified life, to the Dutch it is a matter of relieving boredom.

From chapter III, of the Netherlands National Report to UNCED 1992; National policies and implementation

*The government publication Nature Policy Plan 1990 examines the interac-*tion between the natural environment and society. The Nature Policy Plan is an attempt to give shape to Dutch domestic and international policy in this area, taking this interaction into account. Government policy is based on the following key elements:

1. Ecological superstructure
Efforts will be made to create a sustainable structure for the natural environment in the Netherlands. The country still has many unique ecological features. If these features are to be sustainably maintained, restored and developed, an ecological superstructure – comprising a cohesive network of existing and planned significant natural areas – is essential. This superstructure would be made up of key areas, nature development areas and connective zones.

Key areas
Key areas are natural areas, country estates, woodland areas, large bodies of water and valuable old agricultural landscapes. Existing ecological features would be conserved and developed.

Nature development areas
Nature development areas are those areas which lend themselves to the development of ecological features of national and/or international importance. More than in key areas, the emphasis here is on changing land use and land redevelopment.

Ecological corridors
Ecological corridors are areas which link key areas and nature development areas. They are important in that they improve the distribution of and contacts between animals and plants.

Species policy
Attempts are being made to conserve or restore a number of animal species in the Netherlands. Species policy is partially geared to areas outside the ecological superstructure and aims to promote research and the dissemination of knowledge. "Use" of animals (for hunting, for example) remains possible on a limited scale.

2. General ecological and landscape features
General ecological features include plant and animal species which are found nationally or regionally. "Green belts" in rural and urban areas are essential. In the planning period, a number of projects will be carried out which concern general ecological features.

3. Policy on the countryside
The government has selected a number of areas which are of national and international importance in terms of cultural heritage, geographical significance and scenic value.
The character of these areas must be preserved in order to prevent the Dutch landscape from becoming monotonous.

4. Support for policy on nature and countryside
The government is responsible for policy on features of national and international ecological and scenic importance. Features of regional and local importance are the responsibility of the provincial and municipal authorities. The Nature Policy Plan will have repercussions in other policy areas, including agriculture, infrastructure, earth removal, defence, open air recreation and many other social activities. If the targets of nature policy are to be reached, the support of those who control and use the land is essential. The Dutch Government intends to support private initiatives concerning policy on nature and the countryside. Education on the natural environment and environmental issues in general is also an important means of strengthening public support for nature policy.

This narrow view of nature is translated in the whole way of life. Things are developed partially, even the human senses are developed partially, divorced from one another. It is said human being naturally have six senses. For the Dutch it seems the most important is the optical sense. What is seen is very important.

Almost everything is created for the look. The beautiful shaped and coloured flowers that have no smell; the big and spotless vegetables that have no taste; beautiful landscapes without any internal harmony. Along this line a wonderful example is the small town of Boxtel. As one steps out of the station it is as if one is walking into a beautifully landscaped pigsty minus the pigs. The smell of rotting animal dung is very strong in the air. In this case, it would be sensible to follow the pursuit of the Dutch, living in this would be advisable to put ones sense of smell on the shelf.

Reading all the literature on the conditions of the environment in Holland, one becomes more and more aware of the deterioration of nature behind this facade of human created beauty. Because of this narrow and compartmentalized view of nature it is not surprising if humans get the false feeling of being in control. And the realization that in actual fact humans are not in control becomes almost impossible to accept.

A good example is the greenhouse effect problem. The Dutch should reduce the emissions of carbon dioxide by 80 to 90%, but they felt confident to bargain for 20% and even reduce this bargain to a mere 3-5% by the year 2000.

From a holistic point of view, this behaviour is rather comic, but also miserable. It is not possible to bargain with nature, for it does not care for profit.

Dutch environmental movement: towards sustainability?

Faced by many national and global – so-called – environmental problems the Dutch government and NGO movement propose solutions towards a – so-called – sustainable development.

For both, sustainable development is as defined in the Brundtland Report.

However, both propose to arrive at a sustainable development in different ways. While the Dutch government still strongly believes in economic growth as a precondition for sustainable development, the NGOs put more stress on economic stability and equity, and a smaller claim on a shrinking ecoscape. This will mean that rich countries will have to learn to live on less. Although in the final analysis it is doubtful wether they are actually moving in this direction.

As defined in the Brundtland Report, "Sustainable development is development that meets the needs of the present without compromising the ability of future generations to meet their own needs." This is also the definition the Dutch government subscribes to. How it is translated into policy is interesting.

The Ministry of Development Cooperation's document *A World of Difference* lays down some impressive arguments about the issue in relation to the rest of the world.

"The increase in economic scale and acceleration of technological development have resulted in such world-wide interdependence and mutual vulnerability that a new common ordering of relations is inevitable. At least it must be considered inevitable if the goal is greater stability and less inequality in this world." (page 15).

Further on it is stated that unless rich countries begin to be more serious about their own policies, developing countries will not subscribe to international agreements on problems they believe have their roots in the North.

Here the Dutch government seems to be facing some problems, for although the Netherlands National Environment Plan agrees: "That environmental policy needed to be stepped up in a number of respects in order to be able to realise as quickly as possible the suitable development objectives of the NEPP, ... if not leaving environmental problems to be solved by future generations can only be solved if present patterns of production and consumption are altered. This requires a departure from the existing trend in our behaviour."

However, all actions are geared towards technological solutions, which will make is possible to not change trends of behaviour or the so-called Dutch life style.

J.H.M. Pieters, during an interview at the Ministry of Housing, Physical Planning and Environmental Management, when questioned how balancing North and South corresponds with this continuous search for hi-tech as a solution to environmental problems, stated that with hi-tech the Dutch will still be able to maintain its productivity and thus still compete on the world market, while solving the environmental problems. It will also still be able to import raw materials from Third World countries who badly need the revenue. Reducing imports from the Third World would be detrimental for those countries' development. In the interview, it was clearly stated that it is industrial side effects that need to be controlled, not growth. The issue of a fair price for Third World exports was politely disregarded.

Mr. H. van der Kooi, from the Ministry of Agriculture, Nature Management and Fisheries also stated the same concern for the importance of being able to compete on the world market, while searching for a more sustainable mode of agriculture. Because of this, technological solutions were seen as being more profitable than turning to organic farming, the overall objective of agricultural policy being to foster safe, competitive and sustainable agricultural practices.

At a first glance, there is a very fundamental difference in the policy document written by Mr. Jan Pronk, the minister of Development Cooperation, from what is stated in the policies of both ministries quoted above. While Mr. Pronk proposes more equality to be able to solve the global environmental crises, these two ministries are geared towards competing on the world market for profit. Whether world balance can or cannot not be created through competition is a matter that ought to be discussed.

But this is not to surprising, considering that Pronk himself

Construction work on the offices of the Ministry of Housing, Physical Planning and the Environment (VROM). (Photo Bert Houweling/HH)

is still not clear of how this balance should be created. As the Alliance for Sustainable Development put it:

"Pronk recognises the importance of "autonomy" of labour-intensive, capital-extensive industry. However, in the same breath, he explicitly opts for integration in the world market, a radical liberalization and modernization of production.

Pronk opts for a greater role for international business and the domination of western institutions linked to it. He supports a far-reaching domination of the market, defined by the West, and in the same breath, argues for an increase in the participation of the South. The contradictory aspect of these two basic principles was not even recognized.

The concrete policy is ambiguous in content, and lacks self criticism. The detailing of the concrete policy is in fact formulated without referring back to the framework of policy already worked out."

While in his general analysis of global environmental problems Mr. Pronk points out the hard problems and realities, his proposed solutions are soft to the North and once again it is the South who must change, aided by the Development Co-operation budget of 1.5% of the Dutch National Income.

Development geared towards competition for profit on the world market and the development of high technology avoiding the question of changes in life style could in no way be sustainable at the same time. It could not even meet the standards of sustainability the Brundtland Report demands of not burdening future generations. A good example of this is the proposed solution of saving the soil, air and water in agricultural endeavours. Efforts will be made to create "closed loop" systems whereby the soil, air and water are virtually or entirely free of burden. Non-soil-based systems such as market gardening, under glass mushrooms, cultivation are almost entirely based on monocultures and are therefore subject to a high risk of disease and plague. Large amounts of chemical pesticides and fertilizers are therefore used. In view of the environmental burden by the year 2000 production in this sector will have to be in virtually a closed-loop system (see the Netherlands National Report to UNCED). This policy does not take into consideration the well known fact that the use of pesticides on crops will also result in traces of pesticide residue in the products and how this will have impact on all the Dutch children who consume the products.

Dutch NGOs: killing the pain, ignoring reality.

The Dutch NGO movement in a holistic sense has many very strong elements, but also some weak qualities. This means the movement needs to be strengthened. Within a portion of the movement, some very highly valuable principles have been internalized. These are the six principles of sustainability:

1. The principle of the cultural and social integrity of development. It means that development must grow from within, not be added from the outside.
2. The ecological principle. Development must be compatible with and restore diversity and rely on sustainable forms of resource use.
3. The solidarity principle. Development must provide the basic necessities of life and secure living conditions for all people, promote equity and avoid unequal exchange.
4. The non-violent principle. Development must be peaceful both in the direct sense (the physical violence) and the structural sense (violence embodied in the institutions of the society).
5. The emancipation principle. Development must foster self reliance, local control over resources, empowerment and participation by the underprivileged and marginalized and opportunities for action people can feel is fulfilling.
6. The principle of error friendliness. Development must allow for mistakes, without endangering the integrity of the immediate ecosystem and resource base.

Although it is stressed that a sustainable development must adhere to all six principles and that acknowledging one or two is not enough, a holistic perspective is lacking. This in the end results in partial and specialized action which often fails to address the basic cause of the problems sighted.

One outstanding example of this partial vision is the

Hunger is Not Necessary (Honger Hoeft Niet) campaign. This is a very impressive campaign that also gives its supporters quite a good understanding of how the problem of hunger arises. Citing the debt crisis, it also encourages people to invest in a more "sustainable" way. But is seems to forget to look at the other side of the coin. Its vision is partial, stating that it is only hunger and poverty which need to be fought. A holistic view on the other hand would recognize that you cannot fight poverty and hunger without fighting affluence and overeating. This is where the Dutch life style should come into question.

Joining in a campaign against hunger by donating 10 guilders or more, or investing money in a "sustainable" bank, gives an illusive feeling of goodness, as if one has really helped to alleviate the inequalities in this world (17.000 people give money to Honger Hoeft Niet). Underneath this lies the stubborn disregard of the fact that the problem is the accumulation in the North of riches it needs to support its life style. This point should be addressed at the same time.

The whole slogan "Hunger is Not Necessary" is deceiving. If the life style in the rich countries is to be maintained at the current standard, than hunger is necessary.

The question of life style was often the central issue in many of our – short – discussions. It is worrying to understand that many of our Dutch counterparts are subtly avoiding the issue when it comes to formulating their concrete policies and actions. Instead, much time and energy and money go into elaborate activities that treat the symptoms of "nature's disease", while avoiding the central causes of it. There are many environmentally friendly, hunger friendly, atmosphere friendly, and even Third World producer friendly campaigns. But few are nature friendly in a holistic sense. It is like trying to cure cancer by giving a pain killer!

Addiction of affluence

In a sense, you could say the Western civilization and its Northern peoples are living a hopeless case of drug addiction. No matter how clearly you communicate to them that their behaviour is destructive to themselves and also to others, they cannot control it. They just keep on taking more and more, unless they are forcefully restrained.

In Holland, for instance, politicians, NGO-activists and the public in general have a high awareness of the global environmental problems we face today. All government policy documents concerning the issue stress the need for different patterns of consumption and production, a real behavioural change. NGOs point out the need of more equality, that the people in the North should learn to live on less. Even a multinational corporation policy maker from Shell admitted the problem of life style in the North. But when it comes to the crunch of formulating real action targetting changing the life style, all parties back up. The question which arises is: why is this so?

Many government policies admit without any effort that it is not possible to ask people to change overnight. Yet, government officials announce their optimism prompted by the fact that over the last 15 years people have become much more aware of environmental problems, while overlooking to what degree affluence has also increased in these same 15 years.

The NGOs, on the other hand, are more heterogeneous in explaining their reasons. A very strong underlying variable seems to be the fact that Dutch culture does not allow for too much difference. Being radical is not favoured, even if it is radical action which is needed. As one activist stated, it is money, fashion, etiquette, and group behaviour that rule mentality in Holland. These NGOs are afraid that if they appear too different from the public, they would become too distant, which would ultimately mean no discussion and thus no change at all.

To avoid this situation, many environmental campaigners

Sami Songanbele discusses cattle farming with a Dutch farmer.
(Photo Ruud Gort)

start with small steps, hoping the momentum will naturally move several steps further. As one wishful agriculture campaigner puts it: "When consumers ask for more organic produce, it will be possible to produce more," stating with full conviction that the market system is not the problem.

The unquestionable acceptance of the market system encourages campaigners to search for profitable organic agricultural products in order to coax farmers to adopt organic farming. At the same time, this approach totally disregards the fact that the way the market system works currently gives a very high level of profit to the farmers in the North compared to the farmers in the South.

Jan Juffermans from De Kleine Aarde, together with many

other people, believes that real radical change should occur. Proposing an experimental approach as being the most effective instrument of change, in which all wrong incentives such as subsidies for the car user, agricultural products and so on are removed. When asked whether this is not in fact taking the responsibility out of the hands of the people, he replied that it is the only way for speedy change, acknowledging the fact that to change behaviour a long and difficult process is needed.

In summary the analysis of the global environmental crisis is clear to the majority of the Dutch NGO movement. Fundamental steps towards the change which should be taken are also quite clear. But there is still insufficient acceptance of the reality the changes would demand in the lives of people in the North. There is still a great degree of wishful thinking, as if time could be bought and some pleasant solutions could be worked out. No serious thought has been put into operationalizing the hard solutions these hard problems demand.

At this point anyone can feel great empathy with the Netherlands. How hard it must be to convince yourself that less can be more satisfying when your whole life experience dictates that the more you have the more satisfied you can be.

The Southern vision can only stress the fact that a change in the life style of the North is necessary for sustainable development to be realized. The more this issue is circled about and avoided, the more time is wasted in attaining sustainability. In short, sustainability in the Netherlands will never be possible without this sacrifice.

Chapter 5

Can Dutch society put limits on itself?

Progress and Regress[1]

The environmental crisis in the Netherlands has exposed the fundamental contradiction and dilemma of progress in the West. The regressiveness of progress is very vocal and visible in that country, for example:

Although one of the top producers of farm products with a high rate of productivity, its soil is among the most polluted as a result.

It has the high ratio of eight animals per person. Animal dung is one of the national environmental problems: about 60,000 kg of dung is produced per year per individual which gives a proportion of 6.8 kg of dung per person per hour!

It has one of the highest purchasing powers; every person produces 3,000 kg of household waste per year and waste disposal has become a major national problem.

There are almost 6 million cars for just about 15 million people, and six motorized instruments in every household; all heavily contributing to the greenhouse effect and the depletion of the ozone layer.

Industrial development has reached its zenith; but it has poisoned the air and water.

The list goes on and on. Progress is reflected in the creation of goods, services and luxuries while there is a simultaneous regress on other accounts. Regress is the inevitable other side of the proverbial coin of modern progress. Sandwiched between progress and regress Western civilization, and the Netherlands in particular, seems to be in a mortal dilemma. At every step it takes towards what it calls order, it creates more disorder at levels beyond human control and comprehension.

Making economic behaviour the centre of one's life is the result of the absence of the recognition that the human being's inner resources are the fountain-head of happiness. The reason the level of material build-up and consumption is continuously increasing at an exponential rate can be found in the belief that the inner self can only be enriched through external inputs. Secondly, in the Western view man is the master of creation, out to conquer everything. Not only that, but nature is the adversary of man, to be tamed, commanded and consumed.

These seem to be the determinant traits of a civilization that makes violence its central principle. When economic life has no purpose other than self-propagation, and the purpose of life becomes economically defined and determined, nothing but destruction remains in store.

But Western society, the North, is now recognizing this and it has the capacity to create instruments for self-correction. Coming from the South one is pleasantly surprised to find among Dutch people a growing awareness of this. Take for example the following passage from *A World of Difference:* [2]

"The economic system that followed the industrial revolution and the economic theory that goes with it did not, however, emerge from a vacuum. They reflect value patterns that have formed in Western society. Of relevance in this context are the image of man outside nature, as the man as the master and manipulator of nature, the denial of the intrinsic value of nature and the idea that well-being depends on constantly increasing material welfare."

And it concludes: "The radical changes of policy that will be needed ... must be accompanied by a change in value patterns. There is perhaps a great deal to be learned from what remains of non-Western cultures. This too will give development cooperation a new purpose."

What the Dutch people can probably learn from "what

remains of" non-Western civilizations is how to put limits on so called progress. Whether any society is capable of teaching the Dutch or Europeans remains to be seen, because at present many of them, through their ruling classes, have resolved to violate those limits themselves and to follow in the footsteps of the West. As a consequence they have become even more weak and decadent. Nonetheless it is true that while many societies have contracted this almost fatal disease at the level of their polity and as part of their practice, they are still sound in their philosophies of life, *i.e.* in thought and in certain areas of traditions. Whereas Western societies are based on unsustainable thought, unsustainable policy and unsustainable life style, *i.e.* practice, West is unsound, unsustainable on all the three levels due to the fact that there is a consistent unity among its thought, policy and practice. They are all unsustainable because violence is unsustainable, violence of the western life style is a reflection of its policy and thought which have created spare and image only of a violent, immoral individual. It's very paradigm is unsustainable.

In the midst of all this, civilizations like India, China, and many Asiatic, African, and Latin American countries still remain immovable at the level of the essential nature of their historical heritage. Due to colonial aggression and education its polity was transformed and thus a part of the cultural practices of their peoples.

The realization of this deeper problem has come to the Dutch people through the environmental crisis, and by their own volition they will have confronted the moral problem of their life style and philosophy of life and will have thus invited such policy steps which put limits on "progress".

This would, in the first place, require the wisdom to re-evaluate, from the point of view of sustainability and equity, locally and globally, their relationship with the machine. The "machine-age" appears to be an anathema to sustainability. Indians – of Asia and of America – Arabs, Muslims, Africans,

The production at Volvo-car. (Photo René de Wit/HH)

Latin Americans, Chinese – all knew how to invent machines; but instead kept their hands and feet superior to machine.

Every society developed machines according to their needs. While doing so they made sure that machines were only a help to society's creative and innovative skills. In no way should machines be allowed to replace man's creative use of his own skills in the act of production. Production also involves making moral decisions at every stage. By replacing man with machine modern society has suppressed the creativity of a whole people and allowed production systems to degrade into an immoral system. Devoid of moral judgement and creativity, man has become slave and the economic system plunderer.

Through the use of their hands, which has been idealized by many great men like Tolstoy, Gandhi, Ruskin and Thoreau in their concept of "bread labour", human beings remain rooted in the soil, harmonious with nature as well as with other fellow beings. To take the fullest work from our body – which is fed thrice a day – is the truest celebration of the spirit of human body. It is both a celebration of nature and the body as the body is a part of nature. Those who work with their hands can not become violent and exploitative. No one has to teach moral conduct to people who earn their bread by the sweat of their brow.

An unlimited expansion and growth of the machine has rendered men and women of the North and so of the Netherlands hollow and purposeless. Besides this, it has put an unlimited capacity to steal wealth and labour from others into their hands. They have the unlimited capacity to steal their essential freedom.

The problem of waste, viewed in the reports as a question of disposability, should be seen first as the result of hoarding. Every human being in the Netherlands is a waste-producing factory – they individually produce as much waste as small factories do in the so called "energy-inefficient" Third World countries.

Making the decision to put ceilings on progress

A change of mind towards sustainable development and equity among nations cannot happen overnight. Particularly when commitment to machines, market and progress is blind, both equity and sustainability are impossible, for they have flourished not by a divine force behind them, but by sheer unequal power relations between the North and the South. The foundation was laid through colonization. Therefore to be moral and equitable requires a deep inquiry into the contribution others have made to European progress as well as into Western knowledge systems and its world view. Evaluation of the role of the machine in Dutch life is necessary to awaken the sense of justice and moral conduct and also to increase the areas in which hands, feet and brains can conduct functions.

In an important sense it is not only government and NGOs

but Dutch people themselves who have taken the intellectual initiative among the Northern nations to spell out the degrading impact of their thought, life style and wealth. They should also courageously translate it into action, behaviour patterns and intellectual reforms.

The education of the young is fundamental for the development of long term change in attitudes. By this education we also mean hearing the voices and yearnings of the young. In positively responding to the moral urge of the young ones, Dutch society might within a couple of decades be able to make a real change. Similarly, a high civil sense among the people could be a positive asset in the armoury of change. Maybe citizens' groups can be organized to involve citizens in the exercise of working out a list of things they can and of what they should do away with in their personal, household and social life. For example organizations like Milieudefensie, De Kleine Aarde, NIO and many others are engaged in consumer education and campaigns which have shown positive results.

At the level of alternative thought there are some radical thinkers, like the group at Aktie Strohalm in Utrecht, questioning the very premises of modern economic theories. Similarly in the academic field we see young people and teachers trying to decipher the meaning of environmental crises and also its international linkages. In the media environment is a live issue, and in the political decision making there are traces of new thinking as evident in NEPP and Netherlands National report for UNCED 1992, while the Ministry of Development Cooperation is able to make a considerable radical stride in spelling out the nature of the problem. Among policy makers and civil servants one also finds positive appreciation of the radicals amongst the environmentalists. There is also among civil servants a certain questioning of the relationship between life style and sustainability as we witnessed in talks with Mr. Suurland at the Ministry of Environment, and his colleagues, and with Mr. Pieter Lammers at the Ministry of Development Cooperation. Similarly one witnesses growing debate among Dutch NGOs about the questions of environmental equity and strong self-criticism, as expressed, for example, by Mr. Bram van Ojik of NOVIB and many others. At an intellectual level the conditions for change, one feels, are being worked on. Or, at least there is a growing awareness about the unsustainable paradigm of the West coupled with humility and openness.

Politically, how far the cherished consensus model of governing can be marshalled to effect urgent changes with the speed it requires, remains in the minds of many a question, as expressed for example by Teo Wams of Milieudefensie. On the other hand, Prof. Gerd Junne at the University of Amsterdam feels that if the model is slow at decision making it is secure in providing sustainability to any change that is finally effected. In relation to the farmers it seems that they are becoming rather anxious about the future as they do feel that they, being weaker politically than the industrialists, are being targetted for change. However, groups like the Low External Input Agriculture are confident that a lot of structural changes could be triggered off if the policy of waste being the problem of the producer is carried out. There is extensive expertise in that area and people like Coen van Beuningen are able to effectively explain how such a source-oriented measure can help create conditions for local self-reliance.

In a climate of coalition governments of conservatives, liberals, social democrats, and radicals, radical reforms can certainly be conceived intellectually. Their political delivery would require a strong midwife in the form of a cultivated and articulate public opinion. At the level of public opinion on alternative life style the example of De Kleine Aarde and its relationship with the people of Boxtel is a worthy example.

However, public opinion which has judged the environmental problem as the top priority area is not an indicator of their readiness to make any sacrifices. Prof. Midden of the University of Nijmegen thinks that environmental awareness among Dutch people could not be counted as a sound resource for any radical change. They are willing to deposit their bottles and waste-paper for recycling, but they are not willing to change from private cars to public transport in the same fashion and with similar social enthusiasm. However, perhaps, as some feel, the very physical limitations such as the difficulty of parking cars and the inconvenience of traffic jams, or the ever-intensifying stench of dung and ammonia may ultimately prove to be the effective resources for change.

Socially, Dutch society is as atomised as other European societies – probably more – to "freedom" provided by wealth and welfare mechanisms. Such societies are structurally a great burden on resources, because family does not exist in the way it is institutionalized in many Southern societies. Thus, on the average, for every set of three persons – man, woman and their child – an independent set of all the goods and facilities – house, car, refrigerator, washing machine, TV sets, radios and VCRs, childrens's toys and toiletries, kitchen wares and cooking ranges, etc. etc. are needed. Besides this purely materialistic aspect of the family, its role is much too extensive and meaningful at a deeper cultural level. Family, clan and community function as counterpoints to the abuse of individualism and freedom. They do not allow these two most fundamental of values to be so abused as they are in the North. These social institutions provide the environment in which one is able to see himself or herself as obligated to others, related to others in a web of obligatory and reciprocal relationships and thus rich in terms of a functional and responsible support structure – to which he/she is also responsible and answerable. These social institutions make an individual internally rich. He is never a lonely individual – ready to break down psychologically at the slightest disturbance – and therefore continuously building up a material world of dead goods around him, to fill the vacuum within, running after a mirage.

We must realize that we cannot handle social problems of that nature by technological modernization and/or mere austerity in resource consumption. Most of the environmental activists and thinkers fall in the same trap of economism which has created and aggravated this crisis. The positive and enriching transformation of the economic man into a meaningful social being is possible by orienting him towards newer dispositions than the economic one. Therefore the real challenge lies in creating a new institutional framework so that the society is introduced to new dispositions. The inner urge then will generate a tremendous energy so that the society will fully open up to them. If inner richness of life is thus restored, outward greed will automatically be controlled and hedonism will be replaced by festivity which is celebrated in interaction and social relationships.

While the South has shown excellence in building up social institutions, the North has shown excellence in building up civil institutions. It is precisely because of strong civil institutions that the Western people have been able to bring order into otherwise a situation of free-for-all. In this sense, North and South can enrich each other by mutually learning each other's excellence.

At the level of faith, a general absence of a strong source of moral authority is always very apparent in the North to Southerners coming from societies in which there is a living tradition of moral and spiritual authority. Such authority is vested by the society in persons of high spiritual attainments, and in persons who have made great sacrifices and who have given selfless service. Moreover, more than individuals, it is traditions, faiths, sects and religion which provide guidance for moral conduct. How far Christianity holds moral authority over Dutch people is questionable. One of the so-called pillars of Dutch society has been Christianity, but lately the pillars and supports rooted in religious faith have been shaken. Ironically, that has come at a time when Christians and their institutions have started undergoing an uplifting change. According to Dr. D.C. Mulder, former president of the Council of Churches in the Netherlands, there has been a debate within Christianity on the subject of its assumption that nature is man's kingdom: that man is the master of nature – king of creation. The 1991 World conference of the World Council of Churches in Canberra voted for a New Theology of Creation. Dr. Mulder thinks that this re-religionization of the church is based on Asian and Indian lines. Thus with the re-estimation of the man-nature relationship and bringing to the centre the idea of integrity of creation, environmental issues have become a major subject within the church. However, half of the people have walked out of the church in the Netherlands and the number is still increasing. A large number of people feel that the Church falls short of their expectations regarding philosophical depth and moral guidance.

Thus we see that the church, *i.e.* religion, is slowly being taken over by secular forces while the church is in itself in the process of reform. Nevertheless, it does have a certain moral influence still on a large number of people. Within the background of its historical role, Christianity cannot present us with a convincing promise. Its new realization about creation is the most indicative of a rebirth. It has yet to mature and become capable of providing a system based on non-violence vis a vis creation – including toward other human beings. It will still have to travel further toward a theology of the Divinity of Creation before it can become capable of providing guidance for a moral re-ordering of its society.

The problem also lies in the nature of authority which is vested in law. Through the authority of law the state has taken over all the power and responsibilities of guiding people. It cannot fulfill this responsibility because it only has an indirect and formal relation with individuals. As a result people are unable to evolve their own moral order. Such a moral order always evolves out of a reciprocity of moral guidance and supervision provided within the community. Authority should be so vested in the plurality of institutions that no one of them could ever be able to usurp the autonomy of the individual. In the North it has been either the Church or the State which has tended to centralize power and authority in itself.

Once having accepted the view that life and inner human resources are central to the problem of sustainability, the Dutch society and government should put their minds to research, education, and policy. Present day scientific, techno-logical, economic, and diplomatic instruments, which were created in the service of attaining and maintaining an exponential rate of growth[3] of an extremely extravagant life style and its support system will be of limited use if the Dutch people decide to set new and enlightened goals. These instruments, however, can be used in solving the internal environmental problems as long as there is an equivalent response from the public, as a senior executive of Shell coorporation put it, though for Shell a good public is one which responds to their advertisements!

Since there is a strong lobby within the government and among the NGOs and general public who are concerned with the question of global resource equity and are critical of the "end-of-the-pipe solutions" we venture to point out the meaning and implications of a commitment to sustainability as a way to new paradigm.

Thus, if we relate this and the consumption standards of the Dutch people, and that of the North in general, to environmental disorder and destruction, the language of interpretation of welfare and development must also undergo a radical transformation. Language of development is no different than the language used in the earlier centuries by the Europeans for the political, cultural and spiritual conquest of non-white races. "Enlightenment", "upliftment", "backwardness", "barbaric", "heathens", "fallen", etc. were the standard terms through which the grand mission of "Europeanization", *i.e.* enslavement of non Europeans, was carried out. The ecological disaster alone has returned these terms to Europeans.

The language, the idiom and categories of "progress", of economics, and of science and technology, which was developed in the process and in the service of modern Western industrialization and its political instrument, the nation state, and its Third World edition – development – was essentially designed to meet its goal: achievement of the high level of consumerism in the West and therefore power to the West. You cannot de-consumerize a society while the economic thinking and its system retain the same paradigm, same idiom, same categories and same language.

The Dutch people are mesmerised by the volume of production and they have assumed that control over voluminous produce is affluence. But only a casual perusal shows that they are deprived of what makes life rich, while having plenty of what is peripheraly related to the quality of life.

Therefore the question of life style acquires a new meaning in this context; and the question of sustainability a radical new context and paradigm.

We are faced with a question: What is the language of enrichment? What is the economy of permanence? What is the economy that is moral – for only that which is moral is sustainable in the scheme of nature. West must search for a paradigm which is sustainable – rather than aid the process of whatever exists of sustainable paradigms of non-western people.

Notes

1   For a deeperanalysis of "progress-regress" dilemma see Banwar, *Bharattiy Sanskritiman Van* Hind Swarej Mandal, Rajkot; India, 1991.

2   Pronk, J. *A World of Difference – a new framework for development cooperation in the 1990,* Ministry of Development Cooperation, 1991, p.82.

3   Read for example Willem Hoogendijk *The Economic Revolution,* and Henk van Arkel from Aktie Strohalm *New Prospectives.*

Epilogue

If wealth degrades the environment, as the Dutch case demonstrates, should poverty then wholy maintain it? Looking through the examples of Third World countries the easy answer is no. There one can find many and varied forms of environmental degradation: deforestation, soil depletion, desertification, heavy city pollution. All these have very pressing social consequences, such as ill-health, violence and wars, and worst of all, death striking famines. Thus, it is not difficult to conclude that poverty causes environmental degradation and that this degradation causes further poverty forming a vicious circle, as the Brundtland Report stated. However, the Report is not so explicit on why poverty exists in Third World countries and why so many other visibly poor situations do not disturb the environment. So what we have here is not really a paradox but a mistatement of a political problem that needs to be cleared up.

First of all, neither poverty nor wealth should be considered as self-sustained concepts. On the contrary, they are to be understood as forming one single system so that each one is the immediate and necessary counterpart of the other. Poverty does not mean lack of material goods and wealth the abundance or over-abundance of those goods. They can actually mean lack and abundance only inasmuch as the very same goods are concerned. For a people that do not belong to the same system having less or more of those goods does not have any meaning to them, so they feel no less poor or rich. No one can say that the Mbuti pygmies are poor in food unless they were to come out of their forest and engage in trading forest products for agricultural products with their Bantu neighbours. Otherwise when in their native homeland they live a kind of life that is plenty in itself, with no qualifications. Likewise, no one can say that the Amazonian Urueuuauau Indians, who number less than 1,000 nowadays, are extremely rich because their territory amounts to 1,700,000 hectares, unless that territory is being coveted by timber and mineral companies. Otherwise that territory is only the historical expression of Urueuuauau cultural investment and knowledge. The goods that can be found in that territory are valuable inasmuch as they are given a cultural meaning but they are not accounted an exchange value. The Urueuuauau need that territory as much as the Dutch need to preserve their old and costly seventeenth century buildings, simply because they are cultural assets that play a fundamental part in their identities.

So Third World countries are poor because they belong to a world system where they play the subordinate roles and therefore lack or have only a very small share of the goods that circulate in the system. They are engaged in, if not necessarily committed to, the economic, social, political, and often philosophical standpoints of that system, albeit always in a dominated and low-graded position. It is not poverty that causes damage to the environment but the engagement in the unequal wealth-producing system that does so. As a consequence, it is wealth, and ultimately the concentration of power involved in the allocation of wealth, that causes environmental degradation in the world.

This report reached this conclusion after a seven week long study of environment in the Netherlands and how this environment is perceived, enjoyed and analysed, conceptualized and acted upon by Dutch people, Dutch NGOs and the Dutch government. As it stands it may be considered an encompassing view from the South but we do not claim it to be the all encompassing view. Others could have come to different conclusions, having taken different approaches. Nonetheless we are certain that some of the important points of this much discussed environmental issue in the Netherlands and its interrelatedness to other countries have been elaborated here.

Dutch landscape. (Photo Evert Boeve)

1. Sustainability is not possible without equity

A number of concepts and strategies with a wide range of
market and non-market instruments have been worked out
and are being worked out in the Netherlands to arrive at a
sustainable system both locally in the North and globally. We
have pointed out that these instruments and the very principle
that quick modern society does not allow for the fact that there
is an unequal distribution of wealth and power and therefore
in the world cannot achieve sustainability. Only one minor
half of it "sustains" itself by draining other people's resources
and by it accumulating riches and power and riches over the
rest. Sustainability will only come with equity among nations
and a shift of the West's cherished assumptions about nature,
science and other people's cultural ways.

2. Over-development is the problem

The greatest example of the Netherlands' over-development is the fact, despite its small territorial base, it is the second biggest exporter of agricultural products in the world. To achieve this amazing feat it uses twice as much land from other countries to produce fodder to feed its 120 million animals. The manure produced by these animals is one of the main headaches of the Dutch people, as half of it is lost through leaching and volatilization. The manure pollutes the air, soil and drinking water. The amount of fertilizer and pesticides used in the agricultural sector is enormous. About twenty kilogrammes of toxic materials are used per hectare compared to four kilogrammes per hectare in Germany.

The industry sector is highly energy intensive and is responsible for fifty per cent of total CO_2 emissions. Packaging material wastes are enormous and the incineration of these wastes contribute immensely to the greenhouse effect not to mention its effect as a health hazard.

The mobility of the Dutch population has increased greatly as a consequence of suburbanization and greater prosperity. Fifteen million Dutch possess six million cars in which they spend about seventy four days each year. By 2010 this number is expected to increase to eight million cars with a 35% increase in fuel consumption (RIVM 1988). Traffic is thus a great contributor to acidification, and to the greenhouse effect.

3. Hard problems, hard solutions

At a rational scientific level the Dutch are very clear about the basic environmental problem their country is facing. They also know that the technical fixes available or presumed to be available will not tackle the problems to the point of finding a solution. Consequently they have realized that they need to change their life style in order to cut down on consumption and on energy waste and environmental degradation.

Yet, there is a lack of political and individual will to move in that direction. There is a feeling of self-defeating helpless-ness, avoiding taking any direct responsibility in solving the problem. People, NGOs, and the Dutch government seem to prefer to maintain the status quo by shifting the responsibility for the problem around and into far away institutions like the EC, the UN, the UNCED. It is hard to change one's life style, let alone that of a whole country, but reality dictates the need for hard solutions.

4. Can the Dutch, the North, and the South change their ways?

The world faces an important challenge in the coming years. Nature seems to be tired of coping with so many burdens, and man is beginning to recognize the strain he is putting to nature. At the same time there is too much inequity in the power relations between nations and too much social injustice within. In facing the environmental issue, the North will have to cut down on its life style of over-production and over-consump-tion. The South will have to develop wisely, integrated within the possibilities of its own environment. Thus a sustainable world is called for in which there should be equity, social justice, and respect for nature.

To undertake the task of working together toward these global goals we propose an agenda with the following items. To undertake this task we would have to elaborate an agenda with at least some of the following items:

a. A moratorium on economic growth in the North.
b. A concerted effort toward economic growth in the South during the same period, using environmentally healthy technologies in industry and agriculture.
   The purpose of a. and b. would be to achieve equity among nations through a real economic balance between North and South and a decentralization of power among the geographical regions of the world.
c. Technological and institutional investments in preventing, stopping and recuperating environmental degradation in

the North and the South, including preserving world bio-diversity.

d. Political investments in favour of cultural diversity to counterbalance the hegemony of Western mass culture – also in Northern countries. The movement in the Netherlands and other Northern countries should put much time, thought and even experiment into developing a popular education apparatus to empower people to take the responsibility for change into their own hands, forcing institutions into the direction of addressing the basic problem.

e. The market as an institution – despite the fact that, at this moment, it seems unchallengeable – needs to be rediscussed by intellectuals and thinkers the world over. We refuse to accept that history has stopped at this juncture.

It should be finally pointed out that the holocaust image that the North has been making of the facts of environmental degradation is more a part of their way of thinking and feeling about the world than perhaps a reality in itself. It seems that it is only through such images that Western oriented thought and action tend to move. When fear is the source of inspiration man goes on thinking in terms only of short-sighted, short-term, and what the Dutch environmentalists like to call, "end of the pipe", solutions. It may be possible that end of the pipe thinking is taking away much of the energy that could be used by the imagination and other intellectual resources.

Perhaps it would not be too pretentious to suggest that a concerted effort towards shifting this kind of attitude to a more positive one is an important step which must be taken. Scenarios of nature-oriented systems should be worked out and the search for a deeper dialogue between all parties should be the order of the day.

Bibliography

Alliance for Sustainable Development, "Towards Sustainability; the Netherlands as part of one world. A Dutch NGO *perspective."* Position Paper on behalf of ANPED, Utrecht, July 1991

Netherlands National Report to *UNCED'92*, VROM, July 1991

Netherlands National NGO Report, ADO, July 1991

National Environment Policy Plan (NEPP)

Highlights of NEPP

NEPP Plus

A World of Difference, Jan Pronk

Concern for tomorrow, RIVM, 1989

Environmental Programme: progress report 19, VROM, January 1988

Environmental Impact Assessment: The Netherlands – fit for future life, Dutch Ministry of Environment (VROM) 1990

Acidification in the Netherlands in the the Netherlands – effects and policies, VROM

Indicative multi-year programme to control air pollution 1985-1989, VROM

Waste Substances Act, VROM

Preliminary study into noise emission limits for railway rolling stock in the Netherlands, VROM

The role of ammonia in acidification in the Netherlands, VROM

Recycling and clean technologies, VROM

The perception of energy risks, VROM

Pesticides Act 1962, VROM

Pesticides Decree, VROM

Pesticides Authorization Order, VROM

Order on the composition, classification, packaging and labelling of pesticides, VROM

Netherlands supplementary research programme on acidification, VROM

Regulations concerning protection of the soil (Soil Protection Act), VROM

Directive for the quality of materials and chemicals used for public water supplies, VROM

Netherlands Chemical Substances Act, VROM

Waste – present situation in the Netherlands, VROM

Memorandum on traffic and the environment, VROM

Making the Netherlands a cleaner country, VROM

Environmental hygiene and urban and village renewal, VROM

Netherlands Chemical Waste Act, VROM

Environmental Impact Assessment Decree, VROM

Environmental Policy in the Netherlands, VROM

Environmental Situation in the Netherlands, 1990, The Hague, Netherlands Central Bureau of Statistics

The Netherlands in Brief, The Hague: Foreign Information Service, Ministry of Foreign Affairs, 1990

In search of sustainable agriculture, Berenschot Report, 1990

Netherlands Travelling Clean, Friends of the Earth Netherlands, 1990

Milieu, *Netherlands Journal of Environmental Science,* Volume 5, 1990/6

Henk van Arkel, *New Prospectives for the solution of the Environmental Crisis,* Aktie Strohalm, 1991

Bailey, A., *Letter from the Netherlands,* August 1991

Rob van den Berg "From Research to Results: Present and Future Research from the viewpoint of Development Cooperation", Reprint from *Research and development cooperation:* the role of the Netherlands, C.Schweigman and U.T. Bosma (eds.) Amsterdam, Royal Tropical Institute, 1990

Harle, N. "The ecological impact of over-development: a case study of Limburg," *The Ecologist,* Vol.20 No.5, 1990

Willem Hoogendijk, *The Economic Revolution,* Uitgeverij Jan van Arkel/Green Print, 1991

Ad Koekkoek, Arie Kuyvenhoven and Willem Molle "Europe 1992 and th Developing Countries, an Overview" Reprint from *Journal of Common Market Studies,* Oxford, 1990

Bill McKibben, *End of Nature,* Viking, 1990

Lester Milbrath, *Envisioning a Sustainable Society,* SUNY, 1989

Klarissa Nienhuyis, "NGOs and Energy Policy Change", paper presented at the International Conference "Energy in Central and Eastern Europe", Czechoslovakia, 1991

Michael Renner 1988, *Rethinking the role of the Automobile,* Worldwatch Paper 84